DDC 22
A Practical Approach

By

Dr. Sanjay K Kaushik

M. Lib. & Inf. Sc., Ph. D. (Lib. & Inf. Sc.)
PGDLAN (Hyderabad), APGDIT (Rohtak)
Assistant Librarian
M. D. University,
Rohtak-124 001.
HARYANA

Ess Ess Publications

4837/24, Ansari Road, Darya Ganj,
New Delhi-110002
✆ : 23260807
Fax : 23274173
E-mail: info@essessreference.com
url:http://www.essessreference.com

First Published 2004

ISBN : 81-7000-414-4

Price : Rs.475/-

Published by :

Ess Ess Publications

4837/24, Ansari Road, Darya Ganj.
New Delhi - 110 002
Phone : 23260807
Fax : 23274173
E-mail: info@essessreference.com
url:http://www.essessreference.com

Printed at :
Print Line

Dedicated with Regards to
Late Sh. JAI NARIAN KAUSHIK
The Perennial Source of Inspiration

CONTENTS

PREFACE

Classification is the basis of librarianship. No large library in the world can survive without a library classification scheme. The library classification is also being taught as compulsory subject in the various courses of library and information science allover the World. A system of library classification that flashed across the inquiring mind of young Melvil Louis Kossuth Dewey (known as Melvil Dewey) in 1873 is still the most popular classification scheme. The modern library classification begins with Dewey Decimal Classification (DDC). Melvil Dewey devised DDC in 1876. DDC has its credit of 128 years of boundless success. The DDC is being used in majority of libraries in about 150 countries. Despite the ever-mounting criticism of its faulty approach and the 19th century structure, the popularity of DDC has always shown a spiking graph. No doubt, for a classification system to maintain its relevancy, it must be continually revised and expanded. The DDC has a continuous revision policy. The Decimal Classification Editorial Policy Committee (EPC) is responsible for revisions and expansions in DDC. This is the result of continuous revision that the 22nd edition of DDC has been published in July 2003. No other classification scheme has published so many editions. Some welcome changes have been made in DDC 22. To reduce the Christian bias in 200 Religion, the numbers 201 to 209 have been devoted to Specific aspects of religion. In the previous editions these numbers were devoted to Christianity. The second major change in DDC 22 is the removal of Table 7. To enhance the classifier's efficiency Table 7 has been removed from DDC 22 and the provision of adding group of persons is made by direct use of notation already available in schedules and in notation -08 from Table 1 Standard Subdivisions.

The present book is an attempt to explain with suitable examples the salient provisions of DDC 22. The book is written in simple language so that students may not face any difficulty. The examples in the book are explained in a step-by-step procedure. The first two chapters are devoted to introduction and major changes in DDC 22, respectively. Chapter three is devoted to the schedules. In the chapters four to nine Tables 1 to 6 have been dealt. Groups of persons is dealt in chapter 10. It is hoped that this book will prove of great help and use to the library professionals in general and Library and Information Science students in particular.

The author will accept with pleasure the suggestions or errors or omission about/ in the book noticed and conveyed by the intelligent readers.

I am very much thankful to Dr. (Mrs.) Ashu Shokeen, Chairperson, Department of Library and Information Science, whose constant inspirations made me capable of taking such an assignment as a challenge and no looking behind until the work is complete. I am also thankful to my professional colleagues at M. D. University Library, Rohtak who have cooperated me at every stage. My thanks are also due to my friends and well-wishers whose blessings are always with me.

I cannot express my thanks in words towards my family, especially my mother, wife Mrs. Nishi, daughter Ms. Anshu and son Master Adhav, whose time I have stolen for preparation of this book.

Finally I thank Mr. Sumit Sethi of Ess Ess publishers who have whole-heartedly accepted the work of publication of this book.

Dated: 21st June 2004

Dr. Sanjay K Kaushik
kaush_s@rediffmail.com

1
INTRODUCTION TO DDC 22

MELVIL DEWEY: A BRIEF SKETCH

The deviser of DDC was an American Librarian namely Melvil Dewey, whose full name is Melvil Louis Kossuth Dewey. He was born on 10th September 1851 in the Adms Centre city of New York State. Melvil was a son of small businessman and at the age of five he said I will arrange my mother's larder. In 1870 he took admission in Amherst College for his higher studies and at the age of 23 he got the Bachelor degree in 1874. During his studies in the college he joined the college library as a student assistant and after getting the graduation he was appointed as Assistant Librarian of this college[1]. As student assistant, he prepared a scheme for classifying the books of Amherst College during 1873-75 and got his classification scheme published in the year 1876.

Later Melvil was appointed as Librarian of New York State Library. In 1887 Melvil established the first library science school in Columbia University and started teaching. Melvil also has the distinction of being editor and publisher of the first magazine of library science namely "Library Journal". Apart from this he also played a vital role in the establishment and directing of several institutions like: American Library Association, Spelling Reform Association, Metric Bureau, British Library Association, Readers and Writers company, Library Bureau, etc[2].

On 30th December 1931 the profession of Librarianship had lost this great librarian but the profession will remain indebted forever to this great personality.

Origin and growth of DDC

Melvil Dewey visited a number of libraries before devising his classification scheme. He sought suggestions in this regard from W T Harris, Jacob Schwart and Natale Battezzati. He applied the scheme for experiment to Amherst College Library during 1873- 76 and after its success he published his scheme in 1876. The title of this scheme was "A Classification and subject index for cataloguing and arranging the books and pamphlets of a library". This edition received a warm welcome from American Librarians. The size of first edition was very small. It contained only 44 pages out of which 14 pages were devoted to introduction, 18 pages were devoted to index and only 12 pages were devoted to schedules.

The second edition under the name of Melvil Dewey was brought out in 1885. This edition unlike the first edition had the name of Melvil Dewey as author. The title was changed as "Decimal classification and relative index for arranging, cataloguing and indexing public and private libraries and for pamphlets, clippings, notes, scrapbooks, index, resumes, etc." After the death of Melvil Dewey, in 1951 his name was added to the title and in 15th revised edition title was again changed as "Dewey Decimal Classification and relative index". This title still remains in the 22nd edition published in July 2003.

A brief account of all the editions of DDC is given in the following table[3].

Edition number	Year of publication	Number of volumes	Total pages
First	1876	One	44
Second	1885	One	314
Third	1888	One	416
Fourth	1891	One	466
Fifth	1894	One	467
Six	1899	One	511

Seven	1911	One	792
Eight	1913	One	850
Ninth	1915	One	856
Tenth	1919	One	940
Eleventh	1922	One	988
Twelfth	1927	One	1243
Thirteenth	1932	One	1647
Fourteenth	1942	One	1927
Fifteenth	1951	One	1716
Fifteenth (revised)	1952	One	1927
Sixteenth	1958	Two	2439
Seventeenth	1965	Two	2480
Eighteenth	1971	Three	2692
Nineteenth	1979	Three	4779
Twentieth	1989	Four	3273
Twenty first	1996	Four	4037
Twenty second	2003	Four	3983

Since the publication of its first edition in 1876, the Dewey Decimal Classification (DDC) system has crossed many milestones. Some major milestones are mentioned in the below table[4]:-

Year	Milestones
1876	The first edition entitled "A Classification and Subject Index for Cataloguing and Arranging Books and Pamphlets of a library" is published
1885	The second edition is published under the name of great Melvil Dewey
1900	The first abridged edition of the DDC is published
1916	The Decimal Classification Advisory Committee- the American Library Association's first advisory

	committee- is appointed
1923	The DDC editorial office moves to the Library of Congress in Washington, DC
1930	The Library of Congress begins to print Dewey numbers on catalog cards
1931	The great Melvil Dewey dies
1937	The Decimal Classification Committee is established
1953	The Decimal Classification Editorial Committee is reconstituted to represent the American Library Association (ALA), Forest Press and the Library of Congress to guide to editorial development of the DDC.
1958	The 16th edition of the DDC is published. This edition was edited under agreement between the LC and Forest Press.
1988	Forest Press becomes a division of OCLC
1993	OCLC Forest Press publishes Electronic Dewey, the first library classification scheme in electronic form
1996	The 21st edition of the DDC for Windows are published, making it the first time print and electronic formats are published simultaneously
2000	WebDewey in CORC is published
2002	WebDewey and abridged WebDewey are published
2003	22nd edition of DDC is published

Classifying with the DDC

Classifying a work with DDC requires determining the subject, the disciplinary focus, and if applicable the approach or form.

DETERMINING THE SUBJECT OF A WORK

Classifying a work properly depends first upon determining the subject of the work in hand. A key element in determining the subject is the author's intent. Some tips for determining the subject of a work are as follows.

1. The title is often a clue to the subject, but should never be the sole source of analysis. For example, "Who Moved My Cheese?" is a work on coping with change, not a work related to the culinary arts. Likewise, a title with specific terms that are subdivisions of a field may in fact use such terms symbolically to represent the broader topic. For example, titles containing terms like chromosomes, DNA, double helix, genes, and genomes may use these terms symbolically to represent the whole subject of biochemical genetics.
2. The table of contents may list the main topics discussed. Chapter headings may substitute for the absence of a table of contents. Chapter subheadings often prove useful.
3. The preface or introduction usually states the author's purpose. If a foreword is provided, it often indicates the subject of the work and suggests the place of the work in the development of thought on the subject. The book jacket or accompanying material may include a summary of the subject content.
4. A scan of the text itself may provide further guidance or confirm preliminary subject analysis.
5. Bibliographical references and index entries are sources of subject information.
6. Cataloguing copy from centralized cataloguing services is often helpful by providing subject headings, classification numbers, and notes. Such copy appears in online services, and on the verso of the title page of many U S, Australian, British, and Canadian books as part of Cataloguing-in-publication (CIP) data. Data from these sources should be verified with the book in hand, since the cataloguing record is based on prepublication information.

7. Occasionally, consulation of outside sources such as reviews, reference works, and subject experts may be required to determine the subject of the work.

DETERMINING THE DISCIPLINE OF A WORK

After determining the subject, the classifier must then select the proper discipline, or field of study, of the work.

The guiding principle of the DDC is that a work is classed in the discipline for which it is intended, rather than the discipline from which the work derives. This enables works that are used together to be found together. For example, a general work by a zoologist on agricultural pest control should be classed in agriculture, not zoology, along with other works on agricultural pest control.

Once the subject has been determined, and information on the discipline has been found, the classifier will turn to the schedules. The summaries are a good means of mental navigation. The headings and notes in the schedules themselves and the Manual provide much guidance. The relative index may help by suggesting the disciplines in which a subject is normally treated.

If the relative index is used, the classifier must still rely on the structure of the classification and various aids throughout to arrive at the proper place to classify a work. Even the most promising Relative Index citations must be verified in the schedules; the schedules are the only place where all the information about coverage and use of the numbers may be found.

MORE THAN ONE SUBJECT IN THE SAME DISCIPLINE

A work may include multiple subjects treated separately or in relation to one another from the viewpoint of a single discipline. Use the following guidelines in determining the best placement for the work:

1. Class a work dealing with interrelated subjects with the subject that is being acted upon. This is called the rule of application, and work takes precedence over any other rule.

For instance, class an analytical work dealing with Shakespeare's influence on Keats with Keats. Similarly, class a work on the influence of the great Depression on the 20th century American art with American art.

2. Class a work on two subjects with the subject receiving fuller treatment.

3. If two subject receive equal treatment, and are not used to introduce or explain one another, class the work with the subject whose number comes first in the DDC schedules. This is called the first-of-two rule. For example, a history dealing equally with the United States and Japan, in which the United States is discussed first and is given first in the title, is classed with the history of Japan because 952 Japan precedes 973 United States.

   Sometimes, specific instructions are given to use numbers that do not come first in the schedules. For example, at 598, the note "class comprehensive works on warm-blooded vertebrates in 599" tells the classifier to ignore the first-of-two rule and class a work on birds (598) and mammals (599) in 599, which is the comprehensive number for warm-blooded vertebrates.

   Also disregard the first-of-two rule when the two topics are the two major subdivisions of a subject. For example, collection systems (628.142) and distribution systems (628.144) taken together constitute 628.14 Collection and distribution systems. Works covering both of these topics are classed in 628.14 (not 628.142).

4. Class a work on three or more subjects that are all subdivisions of a broader subject in the first higher number that includes them all. This is called the rule of three. For example, a history of China (951), Japan (952) and India (954) is classed with the history of Asia (950).

5. Subdivisions beginning with zero should be avoided if there is a choice between 0 and 1-9 at the same point in the

hierarchy of the notation. Similarly, subdivisions beginning with 00 should be avoided when there is a choice between 00 and 0. This is called the rule of zero. For ecxample, a biography of an American Methodist missionary in China belongs in 266 Missions. The content of the work can be expressed in three different numbers:

266.0092	biography of a missionary
266.02373051	foreign missions of the US in China
266.76092	biography of a United Methodist Church missionary

The last number is used since it has no zero at the fourth position.

MORE THAN ONE DISCIPLINE

Treating a subject from the point of view of more than one discipline is different from treating several subjects in one discipline. Use the following guidelines in determining the best placement for the work:

1. Use the interdisciplinary number provided in the schedules or relative Index if one is given. An important consideration in using such an interdisciplinary number is that the work must contain significant material on the discipline in which the interdisciplinary number is found. For example, 305.231 is provided for interdisciplinary works on child development. However, if a work that is interdisciplinary with respect to child development gives little emphasis to social development and a great deal of emphasis to the psychological and physical development of the child (155.4 and 612.65, respectively), class it in 155.4 (the first number in the schedules of the next two obvious choices). In short, interdisciplinary numbers are not absolute; they are to be used only when applicable.
2. Class works not given an interdisciplinary number in the discipline given the fullest treatment in the work. For

example, a work dealing with both the scientific and the engineering principles of electrodynamics is classed in 537.6 if the engineering aspects are introduced primarily for illustrative purposes, but in 621.31 if the basic scientific theories are only preliminary to the author's exposition of engineering principles and practices.

3. When classifying interdisciplinary works, do not overlook the possibilities of main class 000 Computer science, information & general works, e.g. 080 for a collection of interviews of famous people from various disciplines.

Any other situation is treated in the same fashion as those found in the instructions at More Than One Subject in the Same Discipline.

TABLE OF LAST RESORT

When several numbers have been found for the work in hand, and each seems as good as next, the following table of last resort (in order of preference) may be used as a guideline in the absence of any other rule:

Table of last resort

1. Kinds of things
2. Parts of things
3. Materials from which things, kinds, or parts are made
4. Properties of things, kinds, parts, or materials
5. Processes within things, kinds, parts, or materials
6. Operations upon things, kinds, parts, or materials
7. Instrumentalities for performing such operations

For example, surveillance by border patrols could be classed in either 363.285 Border patrols, or 363.232 Patrols and surveillance. Choose 363.285 since border patrols are a kind of police services, while patrols and surveillance are processes performed by police services.

Note: Don't apply this table or any other guideline if it appears to disregard the author's intention and emphasis.

NOTES IN DDC 22

To guide the classifier at the point where need is felt, a vertiginous variety of notes are provided in DDC. Notes are important because they supply information that is not obvious in the notational hierarchy or in the heading with regard to order, structure, subordination, and other matters. Notes may appear in the record for a number or a span of numbers. Notes may also appear at the beginning of a table. Footnotes are used for instructions that apply to multiple subdivisions of a class, or to a topic within a class. Broadly these notes are categorized in four categories, which are explained in the following paragraphs:

1. Notes that describe what is found in a class: This category of notes consists of various notes, which tell the classifier to what is to be classified under this class. *Definition notes* indicate the meaning of a term in the heading. For example:

364 Criminology

Crime and its alleviation

This note defines that the documents dealing with crime and its alleviation should be classified under the number 364.

Scope notes indicate whether the meaning of the number is narrower or broader than is apparent from the heading. For example:

005.3 Programs

Software, firmware, middleware

Number-built notes identify and explain the source of built numbers included in the schedules and tables. Built numbers are occasionally included in the schedules or tables to provide additional information or to indicate exceptions to regular add instructions. For example:

353.132 63 Foreign service

Number built according to instructions under 352-354

Class here consular and diplomatic services

Former-heading notes are provided only when the heading associated with a class number in the previous edition has been altered to such a degree that the new heading bears little or no resemblance to the previous heading, even though the meaning of the number has remained substantially the same. For example:

659.131 5 Industrial advertising

Former heading: Advertising directed to vocational uses

Variant-name notes are given for synonyms or near synonyms. For example:

005.746 Data compression

Variant names: data compaction, file compression

Class-here notes list major topics in a class. These topics may be broader or narrower than the heading, overlap it, or define another way of looking at essentially the same material. Topics in class-here notes are considered to approximate the whole of the class. For example:

025.4 Subject analysis and control

Class here standards for subject analysis and control

2. Notes that identify topics in standing room: This type of notes are called including notes. Including notes identify topics that have "standing room" in the number where the note is found. Standing room numbers provide a location for topics with relatively few works written about them, but whose literature may grow in the future, at which time they may be assigned their own number. For example:

005.52 Word processing

Including grammar checkers, spelling checkers, style checkers

3. Notes that describe what is found in other classes: This type of notes lead the classifier to interrelated topics, or distinguish among numbers in the same notational hierarchy. In DDC 22 these notes are provided as class-elsewhere notes, and see and see also notes. *Class elsewhere notes* are used to show preference order, to lead to the comprehensive or interdisciplinary number, to override the first-of-two rule, or to lead to broader or narrower topics in the same hierarchical array that might otherwise be overlooked. An example of class elsewhere notes is as under:

616.891 8 Drug therapy

Class drug stock therapy in 616.891 2

See references lead from a stated or implied comprehensive number for a concept to the component parts of that concept in a different notational hierarchy. A see reference may point to a specific number, or to a concept scattered throughout the schedules. Each see reference begins with the word "For" and appears in italics. For example:

666.3 Pottery

Class here comprehensive works on clay technology

Class pottery in the narrow sense of earthenware in 666.6

For techniques and procedures, see 666.44; for specific types of pottery, see 666.5-666.6; for structural clay products, see 666.73

See-also references lead the classifier to related topics. They are reminders that minor differences in wording and context can imply differences in classification. Each see-also reference appears in italics. For example:

641.87 Preparing beverages

Class interdisciplinary works on beverages in 641.2

See also 641.62 for cooking with beverages

4. Notes that explain changes or irregularities in the schedules and tables: This category also include various notes which bring to the notice of the classifier the changes or irregularities in the schedules as well as tables. Discontinued notes indicate that all or part of the contents of a number have been moved to a more general number in the same hierarchy, or have been dropped entirely. For example:

[653.424 2-.424 5]Isaac Pitman, Benn Pitman, Graham, Munson systems

Numbers discontinued; class in 653.424

Relocation notes state that all or part of the contents of number have been moved to a different number. For example:

[537.67] Quantum electrodynamics

Relocated to 530.143 3

Do-not-use notes instruct the classifier not to use all or part of the regular standard subdivision notation or an add table provision, but instead to use a special provision or standard subdivision notation at a broader number. When the whole standard subdivision is removed from use, the note appears under a bracketed standard subdivision; when only part of the standard subdivision is displaced, the part displaced is specified. For example:

[026.000 68] Management

Do not use; class in 025.19

028.108 Reviews with respect to kinds of persons

Do not use for reviews of works for specific kinds of users; class in 028.16

NOTATION USED IN DDC

In DDC Indo-Arabic numerals have been used to represent each class. The first digit in each three-digit number represents the main class. For example, 300 represents social science. The second digit in each three-digit number indicates the division.

For example, 300 is used for general works on the social sciences 320 for Political science, 330 for Economics. The third digit in each three-digit number indicates the section. Thus, 330 is used for general works on Economics. 331 for Labour economics, 332 for Financial economics, 333 for Economics of land & energy The DDC uses the convention that no number should have fewer than three digits; zeros are used to fill out numbers.

A decimal point or dot is inserted between the third and fourth digit in a class number. This dot is not a decimal point in the mathematical sense, but a psychological pause to break the monotony of numerical digits and to ease the transcription and copying the class number. A number should never end in a zero anywhere to the right of the decimal point.

STRUCTURE OF DDC

DDC-is a hierarchical scheme of classification, which proceeds from the general to the specific. The basic arrangement is by discipline, and a specific subject can occur in any number of disciplines. The universe of subject is divided into ten main classes, which are enumerated in First Summary. Each main class is further divided into ten divisions. These hundred divisions are enumerated in Second Summary. Further each division is divided into ten sections. These thousand sections are enumerated in Third Summary. The hierarchical structure of DDC can be understood by following example:

300	Social science
330	Economics
332	Financial economics
332.1	Banks

OUTLINE OF DDC 22

The DDC 22 is composed of following major parts in four volumes:

Volume 1

1. New features in edition 22: A brief explanation of the special features and changes in DDC 22
2. Introduction: A description of the DDC and how to use it
3. Glossary: Short definitions of terms used in the DDC
4. Index to the Introduction and glossary
5. Manual: A guide to the use of the DDC that is made up primarily of extended discussions of problem area in the application of DDC. Information in the manual is arranged by numbers in the tables and schedules.
6. Tables: Six numbered tables of notation that can be added to class numbers to provide greater specificity
7. Lists that compare Editions 21 and 22: Relocations and Discontinuations; Reused Numbers

Volume 2

1. DDC Summaries: The top three levels of the DDC
2. Schedules: The organization of knowledge from 000-599

Volume 3

1. Schedules: The organization of knowledge from 600-999

Volume 4

1. Relative Index: An alphabetical list of subjects with the disciplines in which they are treated subarranged alphabetically under each entry

SUMMARIES

In volume 2 of DDC 22, three summaries have been provided at pages v to xvi. The First Summary contains The Ten Main Classes. The Second Summary contains The Hundred Divisions and The Thousand Sections are contained in the Third Summary. The students are advised to go time and again through these summaries so that they can become familiar with these summaries. These are provided at next few pages.

First Summary

The Ten Main Classes

000	Computer science, information & general works
100	Philosophy & Psychology
200	Religion
300	Social sciences
400	Language
500	Science
600	Technology
700	Arts & recreation
800	Literature
900	History & geography

Second Summary

The Hundred Divisions

000	**Computer science, knowledge & systems**
001	Bibliographies
020	Library & information sciences
030	Encyclopedias & books of facts
040	[Unassigned]
050	Magazines, journals & serials
060	Associations, organizations & museums
070	News media, journalism & publishing
080	Quotations
090	Manuscripts & rare books
100	**Philosophy**
110	Metaphysics
120	Epistemology
130	Parapsychology & occultism
140	Philosophical schools of thought
150	Psychology
160	Logic
170	Ethics
180	Ancient, medieval & eastern philosophy
190	Modern western philosophy
200	**Religion**
210	Philosophy & theory of religion
220	The Bible
230	Christianity & Christian theology
240	Christian practice & observance
250	Christian pastoral practice & religious orders
260	Christian organization, social work & worship
270	History of Christianity
280	Christian denominations

290 Other religions

300 Social sciences, sociology & anthropology
310 Statistics
320 Political science
330 Economics
340 Law
350 Public administration & military science
360 Social problems & social services
370 Education
380 Commerce, communications & transportation
390 Customs, etiquette & folklore

400 Language
410 Linguistics
420 English & Old English languages
430 German & related languages
440 French & related languages
450 Italian, Romanian & related languages
460 Spanish & Portuguese languages
470 Latin & Italic languages
480 Classical & modern Greek languages
490 Other languages

500 Science
510 Mathematics
520 Astronomy
530 Physics
540 Chemistry
550 Earth sciences & geology
560 Fossils & prehistoric life
570 Life sciences; biology
580 Plants (Botany)
590 Animals (Zoology)

600	**Technology**
610	Medicine & health
620	Engineering
630	Agriculture
640	Home & family management
650	Management & public relations
660	Chemical engineering
670	Manufacturing
680	Manufacture for specific uses
690	Building & construction
700	**Arts**
710	Landscaping & area planning
720	Architecture
730	Sculpture, ceramics & metalwork
740	Drawing & decorative arts
750	Painting
760	Graphic arts
770	Photography & computer art
780	Music
790	Sports, games & entertainment
800	**Literature, rhetoric & criticism**
810	American literature in English
820	English & Old English literatures
830	German & related literatures
840	French & related literatures
850	Italian, Romanian & related literatures
860	Spanish & Portuguese literatures
870	Latin & Italic literatures
880	Classical & modern Greek literatures
890	Other literatures

900	**History**
910	Geography & travel
920	Biography & genealogy
930	History of ancient world (to ca. 499)
940	History of Europe
950	History of Asia
960	History of Africa
970	History of North America
980	History of South America
990	History of other areas

Third Summary

The Thousand Sections

000	**Computer science, information & general works**
001	Knowledge
002	The book
003	Systems
004	Data processing & computer science
005	Computer programming, programs & data
006	Special computer methods
007	[Unassigned]
008	[Unassigned]
009	[Unassigned]
010	**Bibliography**
011	Bibliographies
012	Bibliographies of individuals
013	[Unassigned]
014	Of anonymous & pseudonymous works
015	Bibliographies of works from specific places
016	Bibliographies of works on specific subjects
017	General subject catalogs
018	Catalogs arranged by author, date. etc.
019	Dictionary catalogs
020	**Library & information sciences**
021	Library relationships
022	Administration of physical plant
023	Personnel management
024	[Unassigned]
025	Library operations
026	Libraries for specific subjects
027	General libraries
028	Reading & use of other information media
029	[Unassigned]

030	**General encyclopedic works**
031	Encyclopedias in American English
032	Encyclopedias in English
033	Encyclopedias in other Germanic languages
034	Encyclopedias in French, Occitan & Catalan
035	In Italian, Romanian & related languages
036	Encyclopedias in Spanish & Portuguese
037	Encyclopedias in Slavic languages
038	Encyclopedias in Scandinavian languages
039	Encyclopedias in other languages
040	**[Unassigned]**
041	[Unassigned]
042	[Unassigned]
043	[Unassigned]
044	[Unassigned]
045	[Unassigned]
046	[Unassigned]
047	[Unassigned]
048	[Unassigned]
049	[Unassigned]
050	**General serial publications**
051	Serials in American English
052	Serials in English
053	Serials in other Germanic languages
054	Serials in French, Occitan & Catalan
055	In Italian, Romanian & related languages
056	Serials in Spanish & Portuguese
057	Serials in Slavic languages
058	Serials in Scandinavian languages
059	Serials in other languages

060	**General organizations & museum science**
061	Organizations in North America
062	Organizations in British Isles; in England
063	Organizations in central Europe: in Germany
064	Organizations in France & Monaco
065	Organizations in Italy & adjacent islands
066	In Iberian Peninsula & adjacent islands
067	Organizations in eastern Europe; in Russia
068	Organizations in other geographic areas
069	Museum science

070	**News media, journalism & publishing**
071	Newspapers in North America
072	Newspapers in British Isles; in England
073	Newspapers in central Europe; in Germany
074	Newspapers in France & Monaco
075	Newspapers in Italy & adjacent islands
076	In Iberian Peninsula & adjacent islands
077	Newspapers in eastern Europe; in Russia
078	Newspapers in Scandinavia
079	Newspapers in other geographic areas

080	**General collections**
081	Collections in American English
082	Collections in English
083	Collections in other Germanic languages
084	Collections in French Occitan & Catalan
085	In Italian, Romanian & related languages
086	Collections in Spanish & Portuguese
087	Collections in Slavic languages
088	Collections in Scandinavian languages
089	Collections in other languages

090	**Manuscripts & rare books**
091	Manuscripts
092	Block books
093	Incunabula
094	Printed books
095	Books notable for bindings
096	Books notable for illustrations
097	Books notable for ownership or origin
098	Prohibited works, forgeries & hoaxes
099	Books notable for format

Philosophy & psychology

100	**Philosophy & psychology**
101	Theory of philosophy
102	Miscellany
103	Dictionaries & encyclopedias
104	[Unassigned]
105	Serial publications
106	Organizations & management
107	Education, research & related topics
108	Kinds of persons treatment
109	Historical & collected persons treatment
110	**Metaphysics**
111	Ontology
112	[Unassigned]
113	Cosmology
114	Space
115	Time
116	Change
117	Structure
118	Force & energy
119	Number & quantity

120	**Epistemology, causation & humankind**
121	Epistemology
122	Causation
123	Determinism & determinism
124	Teleology
125	[Unassigned]
126	The self
127	The unconscious & the subconscious
128	Humankind
129	Origin & destiny of individual souls

130	**Parapsychology & occultism**
131	Parapsychological & occult methods
132	[Unassigned]
133	Specific topics in parapsychology & occultism
134	[Unassigned]
135	Dreams & mysteries
136	[Unassigned]
137	Divinatory graphology
138	Physiognomy
139	Phrenology

140	**Specific philosophical schools**
141	Idealism & related systems
142	Critical philosophy
143	Bergsonism & intuitionism
144	Humanism & related systems
145	Sensationalism
146	Naturalism & related systems
147	Pantheism & related systems
148	Eclecticism, liberalism & traditionalism
149	Other philosophical systems

150	**Psychology**
151	[Unassigned]
152	Perception, movement, emotions & drives
153	Mental processes & intelligence
154	Subconscious & altered states
155	Differential & developmental psychology
156	Comparative psychology
157	[Unassigned]
158	Applied psychology
159	[Unassigned]

160	**Logic**
161	Induction
162	Deduction
163	[Unassigned]
164	[Unassigned]
165	Fallacies & sources of error
166	Syllogisms
167	Hypotheses
168	Argument & persuasion
169	Analogy

170	**Ethics**
171	Ethical systems
172	Political ethics
173	Ethics of family relationships
174	Occupational ethics
175	Ethics of recreation & leisure
176	Ethics of sex & reproduction
177	Ethics of social relations
178	Ethics of consumption
179	Other ethical norms

180 Ancient, medieval & eastern philosophy
181 Eastern philosophy
182 Pre-Socratic Greek philosophies
183 Socratic & related philosophies
184 Platonic philosophy
185 Aristotelian philosophy
186 Skeptic & Neoplatonic philosophies
187 Epicurean philosophy
188 Stoic philosophy
189 Medieval western philosophy

190 Modern western philosophy
191 Philosophy of United States & Canada
192 Philosophy of British Isles
193 Philosophy of Germany & Austria
194 Philosophy of France
195 Philosophy of Italy
196 Philosophy of Spain & Portugal
197 Philosophy of former Soviet Union
198 Philosophy of Scandinavia
199 Philosophy in other geographic areas

Religion

200 Religion
201 Religious mythology & social theology
202 Doctrines
203 Public worship & other practices
204 Religious experience, life & practice
205 Religious ethics
206 Leaders & organization
207 Missions & religious education
208 Sources
209 Sects & reform movements

210	**Philosophy & theory of religion**
211	Concepts of God
212	Existence, knowability & attributes of God
213	Creation
214	Theodicy
215	Science & religion
216	[Unassigned]
217	[Unassigned]
218	Humankind
219	[Unassigned]
220	**Bible**
221	Old Testament (Tanakh)
222	Historical books of Old Testament
223	Poetic books of Old Testament
224	Prophetic books of Old Testament
225	New Testament
226	Gospels & Acts
227	Epistles
228	Revelation (Apocalypse)
229	Apocrypha & pseudepigrapha
230	**Christianity & Christian theology**
231	God
232	Jesus Christ & his family
233	Humankind
234	Salvation & grace
235	Spiritual beings
236	Eschatology
237	[Unassigned]
238	Creeds & catechisms
239	Apologetics & polemics

240 Christian moral & devotional theology
241 Christian ethics
242 Devotional literature
243 Evangelistic writings for individuals
244 [Unassigned]
245 [Unassigned]
246 Use of art in Christianity
247 Church furnishings & articles
248 Christian experience, practice & life
249 Christian observances in family life

250 Christian orders & local church
251 Preaching
252 Texts of sermons
253 Pastoral office & work
254 Parish administration
255 Religious congregations & orders
256 [Unassigned]
257 [Unassigned]
258 [Unassigned]
259 Pastoral care of families & kinds of persons

260 Social & ecclesiastical theology
261 Social theology
262 Ecclesiology
263 Days, times & places of observance
264 Public worship
265 Sacraments, other rites & acts
266 Missions
267 Associations for religious work
268 Religious education
269 Spiritual renewal

270	**History of Christianity & Christian church**
271	Religious orders in church history
272	Persecutions in church history
273	Doctrinal controversies & heresies
274	History of Christianity in Europe
275	History of Christianity in Asia
276	History of Christianity in Africa
277	History of Christianity in North America
278	History of Christianity in South America
279	History of Christianity in other areas
280	**Christian denominations & sects**
281	Early church & Eastern churches
282	Roman Catholic Church
283	Anglican churches
284	Protestants of Continental origin
285	Presbyterian, Reformed & Congregational
286	Baptist, Disciples of Christ & Adventist
287	Methodist & related churches
288	[Unassigned]
289	Other denominations & sects
290	**Other religions**
291	[Unassigned]
292	Greek & Roman religion
293	Germanic religion
294	Religions of Indie origin
295	Zoroastrianism
296	Judaism
297	Islam, Babism & Bahai Faith
298	(Optional number)
299	Religions not provided for elsewhere

Social sciences

300	**Social sciences**
301	Sociology & anthropology
302	Social interaction
303	Social processes
304	Factors affecting social behavior
305	Social groups
306	Culture & institutions
307	Communities
308	[Unassigned]
309	[Unassigned]
310	**Collections of general statistics**
311	[Unassigned]
312	[Unassigned]
313	[Unassigned]
314	General statistics of Europe
315	General statistics of Asia
316	General statistics of Africa
317	General statistics of North America
318	General statistics of South America
319	General statistics of other areas
320	**Political science**
321	Systems of governments & states
322	Relation of state to organized groups
323	Civil & political rights
324	The political process
325	International migration & colonization
326	Slavery & emancipation
327	International relations
328	The legislative process
329	[Unassigned]

330	**Economics**
331	Labor economics
332	Financial economics
333	Economics of land & energy
334	Cooperatives
335	Socialism & related systems
336	Public finance
337	International economics
338	Production
339	Macroeconomics & related topics

340	**Law**
341	Law of nations
342	Constitutional & administrative law
343	Military, tax, trade & industrial law
344	Labor, social, education & cultural law
345	Criminal law
346	Private law
347	Civil procedure & courts
348	Laws, regulations & cases
349	Law of specific jurisdictions & areas

350	**Public administration & military science**
351	Public administration
352	General considerations of public administration
353	Specific fields of public administration
354	Administration of economy & environment
355	Military science
356	Infantry forces & warfare
357	Mounted forces & warfare
358	Air & other specialized forces
359	Sea forces & warfare

360	**Social problems & services; associations**
361	Social problems & social welfare in general
362	Social welfare problems & services
363	Other social problems & services
364	Criminology
365	Penal & related institutions
366	Associations
367	General clubs
368	Insurance
369	Miscellaneous kinds of associations

370	**Education**
371	Schools & their activities; special education
372	Elementary education
373	Secondary education
374	Adult education
375	Curricula
376	[Unassigned]
377	[Unassigned]
378	Higher education
379	Public policy issues in education

380	**Commerce, communications & transportation**
381	Commerce
382	International commerce
383	Postal communication
384	Communications; telecommunication
385	Railroad transportation
386	Inland waterway & ferry transportation
387	Water, air & space transportation
388	Transportation; ground transportation
389	Metrology & standardization

390 Customs, etiquette & folklore
391 Costume & personal appearance
392 Customs of life cycle & domestic life
393 Death customs
394 General customs
395 Etiquette (Manners)
396 [Unassigned]
397 [Unassigned]
398 Folklore
399 Customs of war & diplomacy

Language

400 Language
401 Philosophy & theory
402 Miscellany
403 Dictionaries & encyclopedias
404 Special topics
405 Serial publications
406 Organizations & management
407 Education, research & related topics
408 Kinds of persons treatment
409 Geographic & persons treatment

410 Linguistics
411 Writing systems
412 Etymology
413 Dictionaries
414 Phonology & phonetics
415 Grammar
416 [Unassigned]
417 Dialectology & historical linguistics
418 Standard usage & applied linguistics
419 Sign languages

420	**English & Old English**
421	English writing system & phonology
422	English etymology
423	English dictionaries
424	[Unassigned]
425	English grammar
426	[Unassigned]
427	English language variations
428	Standard English usage
429	Old English (Anglo-Saxon)

430	**Germanic languages; German**
431	German writing systems & phonology
432	German etymology
433	German dictionaries
434	[Unassigned]
435	German grammar
436	[Unassigned]
437	German language variations
438	Standard German usage
439	Other Germanic languages

440	**Romance languages; French**
441	French writing systems & phonology
442	French etymology
443	French dictionaries
444	[Unassigned]
445	French grammar
446	[Unassigned]
447	French language variations
448	Standard French usage
449	Occitan & Catalan

450 Italian, Romanian & related languages
451 Italian writing systems & phonology
452 Italian etymology
453 Italian dictionaries
454 [Unassigned]
455 Italian grammar
456 [Unassigned]
457 Italian language variations
458 Standard Italian usage
459 Romanian & related languages

460 Spanish & Portuguese languages
461 Spanish writing systems & phonology
462 Spanish etymology
463 Spanish dictionaries
464 [Unassigned]
465 Spanish grammar
466 [Unassigned]
467 Spanish language variations
468 Standard Spanish usage
469 Portuguese

470 Italic languages; Latin
471 Classical Latin writing & phonology
472 Classical Latin etymology
473 Classical Latin dictionaries
474 [Unassigned]
475 Classical Latin grammar
476 [Unassigned]
477 Old, postclassical & Vulgar Latin
478 Classical Latin usage
479 Other Italic languages

480	**Hellenic languages; classical Greek**
481	Classical Greek writing & phonology
482	Classical Greek etymology
483	Classical Greek dictionaries
484	[Unassigned]
485	Classical Greek grammar
486	[Unassigned]
487	Preclassical & postclassical Greek
488	Classical Greek usage
489	Other Hellenic languages

490	**Other languages**
491	East Indo-European & Celtic languages
492	Afro-Asiatic languages; Semitic languages
493	Non-Semitic Afro-Asiatic languages
494	Altaic, Uralic, Hyperborean & Dravidian
495	Languages of East & Southeast Asia
496	African languages
497	North American native languages
498	South American native languages
499	Austronesian & other languages

Science

500	**Natural sciences & mathematics**
501	Philosophy & theory
502	Miscellany
503	Dictionaries & encyclopedias
504	[Unassigned]
505	Serial publications
506	Organizations & management
507	Education, research & related topics
508	Natural history
509	Historical, geographic & persons treatment

510	**Mathematics**
511	General principles of mathematics
512	Algebra
513	Arithmetic
514	Topology
515	Analysis
516	Geometry
517	[Unassigned]
518	Numerical analysis
519	Probabilities & applied mathematics

520	**Astronomy & allied sciences**
521	Celestial mechanics
522	Techniques, equipment & materials
523	Specific celestial bodies & phenomena
524	[Unassigned]
525	Earth (Astronomical geography)
526	Mathematical geography
527	Celestial navigation
528	Ephemerides
529	Chronology

530	**Physics**
531	Classical mechanics; solid mechanics
532	Fluid mechanics; liquid mechanics
533	Gas mechanics
534	Sound & related vibrations
535	Light & infrared & ultraviolet phenomena
536	Heat
537	Electricity & electronics
538	Magnetism
539	Modern physics

540	**Chemistry & allied sciences**
541	Physical chemistry
542	Techniques, equipment & materials
543	Analytical chemistry
544	[Unassigned]
545	[Unassigned]
546	Inorganic chemistry
547	Organic chemistry
548	Crystallography
549	Mineralogy
550	**Earth sciences**
551	Geology, hydrology & meteorology
552	Petrology
553	Economic geology
554	Earth sciences of Europe
555	Earth sciences of Asia
556	Earth sciences of Africa
557	Earth sciences of North America
558	Earth sciences of South America
559	Earth sciences of other areas
560	**Paleontology; paleozoology**
561	Paleobotany; fossil microorganisms
562	Fossil invertebrates
563	Fossil marine & seashore invertebrates
564	Fossil mollusks & molluscoids
565	Fossil arthropods
566	Fossil chordates
567	Fossil cold-blooded vertebrates; fossil fishes
568	Fossil birds
569	Fossil mammals

570	**Life sciences; biology**
571	Physiology & related subjects
572	Biochemistry
573	Specific physiological systems in animals
574	[Unassigned]
575	Specific parts of & systems in plants
576	Genetics & evolution
577	Ecology
578	Natural history of organisms
579	Microorganisms, fungi & algae

580	**Plants (Botany)**
581	Specific topics in natural history
582	Plants noted for characteristics & flowers
583	Dicotyledons
584	Monocotyledons
585	Gymnosperms; conifers
586	Seedless plants
587	Vascular seedless plants
588	Bryophytes
589	[Unassigned]

590	**Animals (Zoology)**
591	Specific topics in natural history
592	Invertebrates
593	Marine & seashore invertebrates
594	Mollusks & molluscoids
595	Arthropods
596	Chordates
597	Cold-blooded vertebrates; fishes
598	Birds
599	Mammals

Technology

600 **Technology**
601 Philosophy & theory
602 Miscellany
603 Dictionaries & encyclopedias
604 Special topics
605 Serial publications
606 Organizations
607 Education, research & related topics
608 Inventions & patents
609 Historical, geographic & persons treatment

610 **Medicine & health**
611 Human anatomy, cytology & histology
612 Human physiology
613 Personal health & safety
614 Incidence & prevention of disease
615 Pharmacology & therapeutics
616 Diseases
617 Surgery & related medical specialties
618 Gynecology, obstetrics, pediatrics & geriatrics
619 [Unassigned]

620 **Engineering & allied operations**
621 Applied physics
622 Mining & related operations
623 Military & nautical engineering
624 Civil engineering
625 Engineering of railroads & roads
626 [Unassigned]
627 Hydraulic engineering
628 Sanitary & municipal engineering
629 Other branches of engineering

630	**Agriculture & related technologies**
631	Techniques, equipment & materials
632	Plant injuries, diseases & pests
633	Field & plantation crops
634	Orchards, fruits & forestry
635	Garden crops (Horticulture)
636	Animal husbandry
637	Processing dairy & related products
638	Insect culture
639	Hunting, fishing & conservation
640	**Home & family management**
641	Food & drink
642	Meals & table service
643	Housing & household equipment
644	Household utilities
645	Household furnishings
646	Sewing, clothing & personal living
647	Management of public households
648	Housekeeping
649	Child rearing & home care of persons
650	**Management & auxiliary services**
651	Office services
652	Processes of written communication
653	Shorthand
654	[Unassigned]
655	[Unassigned]
656	[Unassigned]
657	Accounting
658	General management
659	Advertising & public relations

660	**Chemical engineering**
661	Industrial chemicals
662	Explosives, fuels & related products
663	Beverage technology
664	Food technology
665	Industrial oils, fats, waxes & gases
666	Ceramic & allied technologies
667	Cleaning, color & coating technologies
668	Technology of other organic products
669	Metallurgy
670	**Manufacturing**
671	Metalworking & primary metal products
672	Iron, steel & other iron alloys
673	Nonferrous metals
674	Lumber processing, wood products & cork
675	Leather & fur processing
676	Pulp & paper technology
677	Textiles
678	Elastomers & elastomer products
679	Other products of specific materials
680	**Manufacture for specific uses**
681	Precision instruments & other devices
682	Small forge work (Blacksmithing)
683	Hardware & household appliances
684	Furnishings & home workshops
685	Leather, fur goods & related products
686	Printing & related activities
687	Clothing & accessories
688	Other final products & packaging
689	[Unassigned]

690	**Buildings**
691	Building materials
692	Auxiliary construction practices
693	Specific materials & purposes
694	Wood construction & carpentry
695	Roof covering
696	Utilities
697	Heating, ventilating & air-conditioning
698	Detail finishing
699	[Unassigned]

Arts & recreation

700	**The arts; fine & decorative arts**
701	Philosophy of fine & decorative arts
702	Miscellany of fine & decorative arts
703	Dictionaries of fine & decorative arts
704	Special topics in fine & decorative arts
705	Serial publications of fine & decorative arts
706	Organizations & management
707	Education, research & related topics
708	Galleries, museums & private collections
709	Historical, geographic & persons treatment

710	**Civic & landscape art**
711	Area planning
712	Landscape architecture
713	Landscape architecture of trafficways
714	Water features
715	Woody plants
716	Herbaceous plants
717	Structures in landscape architecture
718	Landscape design of cemeteries
719	Natural landscapes

720	**Architecture**
721	Architectural structure
722	Architecture to ca. 300
723	Architecture from ca. 300 to 1399
724	Architecture from 1400
725	Public structures
726	Buildings for religious purposes
727	Buildings for education & research
728	Residential & related buildings
729	Design & decoration
730	**Plastic arts; sculpture**
731	Processes, forms & subjects of sculpture
732	Sculpture to ca. 500
733	Greek, Etruscan & Roman sculpture
734	Sculpture from ca. 500 to 1399
735	Sculpture from 1400
736	Carving & carvings
737	Numismatics & sigillography
738	Ceramic arts
739	Art metalwork
740	**Drawing & decorative arts**
741	Drawing & drawings
742	Perspective
743	Drawing & drawings by subject
744	{Unassigned]
745	Decorative arts
746	Textile arts
747	Interior decoration
748	Glass
749	Furniture & accessories

750 Painting & paintings
751 Techniques, equipment, materials & forms
752 Color
753 Symbolism, allegory, mythology & legend
754 Genre paintings
755 Religion
756 [Unassigned]
757 Human figures
758 Other subjects
759 Historical, geographic & persons treatment

760 Graphic arts; printmaking & prints
761 Relief processes (Block printing)
762 [Unassigned]
763 Lithographic processes
764 Chromolithography & serigraphy
765 Metal engraving
766 Mezzotinting, aquatinting & related processes
767 Etching & drypoint
768 [Unassigned]
769 Prints

770 Photography, photographs & computer art
771 Techniques, equipment & materials
772 Metallic salt processes
773 Pigment processes of printing
774 Holography
775 Digital photography
776 Computer art (Digital art)
777 [Unassigned]
778 Fields & kinds of photography
779 Photographs

780 Music
781 General principles & musical forms
782 Vocal music
783 Music for single voices; the voice
784 Instruments & instrumental ensembles
785 Ensembles with one instrument per part
786 Keyboard & other instruments
787 Stringed instruments
788 Wind instruments
789 (Optional number)

790 Recreational & performing arts
791 Public performances
792 Stage presentations
793 Indoor games & amusements
794 Indoor games of skill
795 Games of chance
796 Athletic & outdoor sports & games
797 Aquatic & air sports
798 Equestrian sports & animal racing
799 Fishing, hunting & shooting

Literature

800 Literature & rhetoric
801 Philosophy & theory
802 Miscellany
803 Dictionaries & encyclopedias
804 [Unassigned]
805 Serial publications
806 Organizations & management
807 Education, research & related topics
808 Rhetoric & collections of literature
809 History, description & criticism

810	**American literature in English**
811	American poetry in English
812	American drama in English
813	American fiction in English
814	American essays in English
815	American speeches in English
816	American letters in English
817	American humor & satire in English
818	American miscellaneous writings
819	(Optional number)

820	**English & Old English literatures**
821	English poetry
822	English drama
823	English fiction
824	English essays
825	English speeches
826	English letters
827	English humor & satire
828	English miscellaneous writings
829	Old English (Anglo-Saxon)

830	**Literatures of Germanic languages**
831	German poetry
832	German drama
833	German fiction
834	German essays
835	German speeches
836	German letters
837	German humor & satire
838	German miscellaneous writings
839	Other Germanic literatures

840	**Literatures of Romance languages**
841	French poetry
842	French drama
843	French fiction
844	French essays
845	French speeches
846	French letters
847	French humor & satire
848	French miscellaneous writings
849	Occitan & Catalan literatures

850	**Italian, Romanian & related literatures**
851	Italian poetry
852	Italian drama
853	Italian fiction
854	Italian essays
855	Italian speeches
856	Italian letters
857	Italian humor & satire
858	Italian miscellaneous writings
859	Romanian & related literatures

860	**Spanish & Portuguese literatures**
861	Spanish poetry
862	Spanish drama
863	Spanish fiction
864	Spanish essays
865	Spanish speeches
866	Spanish letters
867	Spanish humor & satire
868	Spanish miscellaneous writings
869	Portuguese literature

870 Italic literatures; Latin literature
871 Latin poetry
872 Latin dramatic poetry & drama
873 Latin epic poetry & fiction
874 Latin lyric poetry
875 Latin speeches
876 Latin letters
877 Latin humor & satire
878 Latin miscellaneous writings
879 Literatures of other Italic languages

880 Hellenic literatures; classical Greek
881 Classical Greek poetry
882 Classical Greek dramatic poetry & drama
883 Classical Greek epic poetry & fiction
884 Classical Greek lyric poetry
885 Classical Greek speeches
886 Classical Greek letters
887 Classical Greek humor & satire
888 Classical Greek miscellaneous writings
889 Modern Greek literature

890 Literatures of other languages
891 East Indo-European & Celtic literatures
892 Afro-Asiatic literatures: Semitic literatures
893 Non-Semitic Afro-Asiatic literatures
894 Altaic, Uralic, Hyperborean & Dravidian
895 Literatures of East & Southeast Asia
896 African literatures
897 North American native literatures
898 South American native literatures
899 Austronesian & other literatures

History & geography

900	**History & geography**
901	Philosophy & theory
902	Miscellany
903	Dictionaries & encyclopedias
904	Collected accounts of events
905	Serial publications
906	Organizations & management
907	Education, research & related topics
908	Kinds of persons treatment
909	World history
910	**Geography & travel**
911	Historical geography
912	Atlases, maps, charts & plans
913	Geography of & travel in ancient world
914	Geography of & travel in Europe
915	Geography of & travel in Asia
916	Geography of & travel in Africa
917	Geography of & travel in North America
918	Geography of & travel in South America
919	Geography of & travel in other areas
920	**Biography, genealogy & insignia**
921	(Optional number)
922	(Optional number)
923	(Optional number)
924	(Optional number)
925	(Optional number)
926	(Optional number)
927	(Optional number)
928	(Optional number)
929	Genealogy, names & insignia

930 **History of ancient world to ca. 499**
931 China to 420
932 Egypt to 640
933 Palestine to 70
934 India to 647
935 Mesopotamia & Iranian Plateau to 637
936 Europe north & west of Italy to ca. 499
937 Italy & adjacent territories to 476
938 Greece to 323
939 Other parts of ancient world to ca. 640

940 **History of Europe**
941 British Isles
942 England & Wales
943 Central Europe; Germany
944 France & Monaco
945 Italian Peninsula & adjacent islands
946 Iberian Peninsula & adjacent islands
947 Eastern Europe; Russia
948 Scandinavia
949 Other parts of Europe

950 **History of Asia; Far East**
951 China & adjacent areas
952 Japan
953 Arabian Peninsula & adjacent areas
954 South Asia; India
955 Iran
956 Middle East (Near East)
957 Siberia (Asiatic Russia)
958 Central Asia
959 Southeast Asia

960	**History of Africa**
961	Tunisia & Libya
962	Egypt & Sudan
963	Ethiopia & Eritrea
964	Northwest African coast & offshore islands
965	Algeria
966	West Africa & offshore islands
967	Central Africa & offshore islands
968	Southern Africa; Republic of South Africa
969	South Indian Ocean islands
970	**History of North America**
971	Canada
972	Middle America; Mexico
973	United States
974	Northeastern United States
975	Southeastern United States
976	South central United States
977	North central United States
978	Western United States
979	Great Basin & Pacific Slope region
980	**History of South America**
981	Brazil
982	Argentina
983	Chile
984	Bolivia
985	Peru
986	Colombia & Ecuador
987	Venezuela
988	Guiana
989	Paraguay & Uruguay

990	**History of other areas**
991	[Unassigned]
992	[Unassigned]
993	New Zealand
994	Australia
995	Melanesia; New Guinea
996	Other parts of Pacific; Polynesia
997	Atlantic Ocean islands
998	Arctic islands & Antarctica
999	Extraterrestrial worlds

TABLES

To provide greater specificity to class numbers, six tables numered Table 1 to Table 6 are provided in volume 1 of DDC 22. The names of these tables are as under :

Table 1. Standard Subdivisions

Table 2. Geographic Areas, Historical periods, Persons

Table 3. Subdivisions for the Arts, for individual Literatures, for specific Literary forms.

Table 4. Subdivisions of individual languages and language families.

Table 5. Ethnic and National Groups.

Table 6. Languages.

Further Table 3 have been divided into three different parts viz. Table 3A, Table 3B and Table 3C. These are discussed in detail in chapter 6.

HOW TO MOVE IN THE SECHDULES

The arrangement of schedules in DDC is according to class numbers starting from 000 to 599 in volume 2 and 600 to 999 in volume 3. Just hold on the volume in right hand and drop the pages, keep your eye on the top of the page you can notice the class number on the top of both sides of the page. The procedure is the same as of consulting a dictionary but the only difference is that dictionary is arranged according to alphabets and DDC is according to Indo-Arabic numerals.

HOW TO BUILD A CLASS NUMBER

The number building process of DDC is a step-by-step process. The simplest way building a class number according to DDC is as under:

Step 1: Select the one of the ten main classes in First Summary, which suits most to your title. In case you have no idea about the title's main class then consult the index (for more details see How to Consult the index? the next heading.)

Step 2: Search among the ten divisions of that main class in Second Summary and select the most suitable one.

Step 3: Search the ten sections of that division in the Third Summary and select the most suitable one.

Step 4: Go to the schedule of that section and search the appropriate number.

Step 5: Write down the base number and, if required, follow the instructions and/ or add standard subdivisions.

Step 6: Insert a dot between the third and fourth digit.

Let us demonstrate this procedure with the help of an example:

Title: Encyclopaedia of Hindu Pilgrimages

Step 1. As is clear from the title that the document belongs to the Hindu pilgrimages. Hinduism is a religion. One of the ten main classes is Religion i.e. 200. Hence we have selected 200.

Step 2. Go to Second Summary under 200, 200 and 210 are devoted to general treatment of religions and 220 to 280 are devoted to Christianity. Hence the only number left is 290 which will cover all the religions other than Christianity.

Step 3. Go to Third Summary under 290, there is a section 294 Religions of Indic origin. Hinduism is of Indic origin. Hence select this number.

Step 4. Go to schedule and consult the notations under 294. Here you will find 294.5 Hinduism.

Step 5. Write down the base number i.e. 294.5. (Please note sometimes the base number given in the add note is different from the number you have written. In this case the base number given in add note is to be written). Go further and you will find an instruction at 294.51-.53. By following this instruction you will go to the schedule under number 201 to 203 and search a number for pilgrimages. Under 203 you will find a number 203.51 Pilgrimages. This number you will write in the rough work portion. From this number now you have to omit the number which have been given between the words "following" and "in" in the add note. Here this number is 20, hence omit 20 from 203.51. Now you will suffix (add at the last of the number) the remaining number to the base number already written. In this case you will add 351. Now you have added number for Hindu and Pilgrimages and your title is encyclopaedia of Hindu Pilgrimages. Go to Table 1 and select a number for Encyclopaedia in Standard Subdivisions. The right choice is -03. (See details in Chapter 4). Add this number at the last of the number built so far.

Step 6. Insert a dot between the third and fourth digit to complete the number. As a matter of convenience give a blank space after every three digits starting from the sixth digit.

The above example will look like this according to the pattern followed in this book:

Encyclopaedia of Hindu Pilgrimages	**294.535 103**
Base Number	294.5
Instruction	Add to base number 294.5 the numbers following 20 in 201 - 203

Pilgrimages	203.51
Encyclopaedia (Table 1)	-03 (s.s.)
	=294.5+351+03
Class No.	294.535 103

HOW TO CONSULT THE RELATIVE INDEX

The relative index is so named because it relates subjects to disciplines. In the schedules, subjects are distributed among disciplines; in the relative index, subjects are arranged alphabetically, with terms identifying the disciplines in which they are treated subarranged alphabetically under them[5]. For example:

Marriage	306.81
arts	700.454 3
	T3C-354 3
customs	392.5
ethics	173
religion	205.63
Buddhism	294.356 3
Christianity	241.63
Hinduism	294.548 63
Islam	297.563
Judaism	296.363
folklore	398.27
history and criticism	398.354
law	346.016
literature	808.803 543
history and criticism	809.933 543
specific literatures	T3B-080 354 3
history and criticism	T3B-093 543
music	781.587
personal religion	204.41
Buddhism	294.344 41

In the above example, marriage as a subject is subarranged under various disciplines and the classifier has to opt for a discipline most suitable to the document in hand. The relative index is primarily an index to the DDC as a system. It includes most terms found in the schedules and tables, and terms with literary warrant for concepts represented by schedules and tables. The relative index is not exhaustive. If the term sought is not found, the classifier should try a broader term, or consult the schedules and tables directly. The classifier should always consult the schedules and tables before he/she applies a number found in relative index.

REFERENCES:

1. Sharma (Pandey S K). Practical approach to DDC: Dewey Decimal Classification made simple. 1998. New Delhi; Ess Ess publications. pp3-4.
2. Gautam (J N) and Niranjan Singh. Dewey Decimal Classification: Practical analysis (Ed. 19 & 20). 1996. Agra; Y K publishers. pp. 1-2.
3. M. D. University, Rohtak. Library Classification: Practice. Lessons for Bachelor of Library & Information Science students. 2003. New Delhi; Excel books. p.8.
4. http:/www.oclc.org
5. Dewey, Melvil. Dewey Decimal classification and relative index. Edition 22. Dublin, OCLC, 2003.

2
MAJOR CHANGES IN DDC 22

Classification is the basis of librarianship. In each library one or another scheme of classification is used. For a classification system to maintain its relevancy, it must be continually revised and expanded. The Decimal Classification Editorial Policy Committee (EPC) is responsible for revisions and expansions in DDC. The 22nd edition of DDC has been published in July 2003. A number of welcome changes have been incorporated in this edition.

NEW FEATURES OF DDC 22

Edition 22nd is claimed to be the first edition of DDC produced in the context of the web environment. The web also enables the OCLC to update the DDC continuously and provide the updates regularly to the users of DDC.

Continuous updating: The continuous updating policy is reflected from the 22nd edition. Since DDC 21 was the first edition published in print and electronic form simultaneously, hence the updates of DDC were used to send through electronic versions and monthly web postings. Dewey for Windows was issued annually from 1996 to 2001. The selected new numbers and changes have been posted on monthly basis since 1997. All of these updates have been incorporated in DDC 22.

New Numbers and Topics: DDC 22 contains many new numbers and topics. These range from new geographic provisions, e.g., the updating of administrative regions in Quebec, to new numbers throughout the DDC for emerging topics in fields such as Computer Science and Engineering, Sociology, Medicine, and History. A number of new built number entries and additional terms have been added to the Relative Index to cover sought topics and provide a wider base of entry vocabulary.

International Cooperation: DDC 22 has benefited from the ongoing advice of the Decimal Classification Editorial Policy Committee and the translator partners. Both groups provide a diverse outlook that is reflected in improvements to terminology throughout DDC 22.

Classifier Efficiency: The major aim of removal of Table 7 and streamlining of the Manual is to promote classifier efficiency. In DDC 22, Table 7 has been removed and replaced by the direct use of notation already available in the schedules and in Table 1 through notation 08. To increase the classifier efficiency each Manual entry has been changed. Apart from this, the information easily accommodated in notes in the tables and schedules has been transferred from the manual, and redundant information already in the schedules and tables has been eliminated from the manual. The Library of Congress Decimal Classification Division DDC application policies previously described in the Manual has been converted into standard Dewey practices. The basic instructions on the use of the DDC have been moved to the Introduction, and background information to Dewey Decimal Classification: Principles and Application. To promote quick understanding and efficient use, the remaining Manual entries have been revised in a consistent style.

MAJOR CHANGES IN DDC 22

In addition to the removal of Table 7 and streamlining of the Manual, there are several major changes in DDC 22. These changes can be discussed under two subheadings as under.

Changes in Tables

Table 2 'Geographic Areas, Historical Periods, Persons' has been updated in DDC 22. To reflect the de-emphasis on race in current scholarship, the name of Table 5 has been changed from "Racial, Ethnic, National Groups" to "Ethnic and National Groups". The provisions for American native peoples and languages in Table 5 and Table 6 have also been greatly expanded. A complete list of relocations, discontinuations, and reused numbers in DDC 22 is available in volume 1 immediately after Tables 1-6 at page numbers 715-731. Some selected changes are provided below:

Table 1. Standard Subdivisions

-029	Commercial miscellany

The subdivisions -029 4, -029 6, -029 7 & -029 9 are discontinued and -029 1 is used for commercial miscellany of area, regions, places in general. The subdivisions -029 3 to -029 9 are reused for commercial miscellany of ancient and modern world. Under these subdivisions add note for use of Table 2 is provided. Hence using the standard subdivision -029 commercial miscellany of any area, regions, places in general and any specific country or continent may be classified.

Table 2. Geographic Areas, Historical Periods, Persons

-23	Collected persons treatment of members of specific ethnic and national groups
-29	Persons treatment of nonhumans

The subdivisions -23 and -29 are new numbers, which are provided to cover persons treatment of members of various specific ethnic and national groups, and nonhumans respectively. Here under -23 add note is given for use of Table 5. Apart from this, in Table 2 a number of subdivisions have been revised / and expanded like: -411-414, -42, -431-436, -437, -438, -44, -451-457, -541-548, -5492, -55, -624-629, -632-634, -648, -669, -6751, -682-687, -71 4, -719, -7287, -85, -861, -883. Some numbers have been relocated like: -54911 relocated from -54912, -549149 relocated from -549142, -5987 relocated from -5986 and -728537 from –728532.

Table 3B. Subdivisions for works by or about more than one author

–30877	Picaresque fiction

This is a new number provided in Table 3B.

Table 3C. Notation to be added where instructed in Table 3B, 700.4, 791.4, 808-809

–377	Magic and witchcraft

This is new number provided in Table 3C.

–32	Places class here travel

The number for travel is relocated from –355

Table 4. Subdivisions of individual languages and language families

-813	Spelling and pronunciation
-89	Use of a spoken language or a manually coded form of a spoken language for communication with and by deaf persons

The above numbers are new in Table 4. Apart from these new numbers, the numbers -31 and –5 have also been expanded in DDC 22.

Table 5. Ethnic and national groups

The first change in Table 5 is the removal of word "Racial" from the name of this table. -05 for Persons of mixed ancestry with ethnic origins from more than one continent have been relocated from -04 and -09 for Europeans and people of European descent have been relocated from -034. In addition to this change -98 has also been revised and expanded. A new number -983 23 is provided for Quechuan (Kechuan) Indians.

Table 6. Languages

The numbers -398 & -98 in this table have been revised/ and expanded. A new number -914 69 for Konkani language has been provided.

Table 7. Groups of persons

The Table 7 has been removed from DDC and a provision of direct use of notation already available in the schedules and in notation -08 from Table 1 is made in DDC 22.

Changes in schedules

Numerous new numbers, relocations, revisions and expansions in the schedules have been provided in DDC 22. These are being discussed as under:-

Computer science, information & general works:- The schedules 004-006 Data processing Computer Science have been completely updated. Certain new numbers like 005.722 Character sets & 006.8 Virtual reality etc. have been included in the schedules. Many relocations have been made such as 005.18 Microprogramming and microprograms is relocated from 005.6, 005.5 General purpose application programs is relocated from 005.3, and 005.52 Word processing is relocated from 652.5. In the main class 070, the title machine-readable publication (070.579 7) has been replaced with Electronic publications (Digital publications) and further expanded to accommodate web publications at number 070.579 73.

Philosophy & psychology: The standard subdivision of psychology .1 Philosophy and theory has been further expanded and two new numbers .198 6 Humanistic psychology and .198 7 Transpersonal psychology have been incorporated. Under .4 Emotions and feelings one new number .44 Guilt and shame has been included. Under Occupational ethics 174 the number .2 for medical profession has been expanded and a provision under .29 has been made to add number following 61 in 610-618 to make the ethics of specific branches of medicine. The numbers .24 & .25 have been relocated to 179.7 & 174.29.

Religion: A two-edition plan was initiated in DDC 21 to reduce the Christian bias in 200 Religion. The rest of the relocations and expansions in 200 Religion outlined in that plan have taken place in DDC 22. In the main class religion, numbers

201 to 209 which were used in the earlier editions for standard subdivisions of Christianity but were discontinued in 21st edition of DDC. These numbers have been used in DDC 22 for covering the specific aspects of religion (viz. mythology, doctrine, public worship, religious experience, religious ethics, leaders and organizations, missions and religious education, sources, and sects and reform movements). The title of number 299 has been changed from other religions to Religions not provided for elsewhere and this number has been expanded at some places like: 299.16 (Celtic religion) to include 299.161 (Specific aspects of Celtic religion). The numbers 299.62, 299.63, 299.64, 299.72, 299.73, 299.74, 299.77, 299.82, 299.83, 299.84, & 299.87 have been relocated to other places.

Social sciences: Under the number 302 Social interactions a new number .231 has been included to cover the digital media. The developments and terminology for social groups and institutions in 305-306 have been updated in DDC 22. Two new numbers viz. 305.235 1 Males and 305.235 2 Females have been incorporated in DDC 22. In main class 320 Political science several new numbers like .546 Black nationalism, .557 Islamic fundamentalism, .558 Black Muslim movement and .58 Environmentalist political ideologies have been included. In main class 330 Economics, the number .155 miscellaneous schools has been expanded and some new numbers viz. .155 2 Institutional economics, .155 3 Chicago school of economics (Monetarism), .155 4 Supply-side of economics, and .155 6 Welfare economics school have been included. The schedule for labor economics 331 has also been expanded and numerous new numbers like: .216 47, .216 49, .252 4, .255 2, .255 4, .256, .257 24, .257 25, .257 27, .257 277, and .257 29 have been incorporated. Many numbers under the main classes 332 Financial economics, 333 Economics of land and energy, and 338 Production have been revised /and expanded. Several improvements to 340 Law have also been introduced that relate to the law of nations, human rights, and intergovernmental organizations. The heading at 341 is changed from "International law" to "Law of nations". Throughout 341, "International governmental organizations" is changed to "Intergovernmental organizations". A topic in either 341.4 or 341.7 that had a corresponding domestic law provision in 342-347 is relocated to the appropriate number in 342-347. The schedules of 342 Constitutional and administrative law, 343 Military ... industrial law, 346 Private law have also been revised /and expanded. In the schedule of educational psychology 370.15, four new numbers viz. 370.152 8 Behavior modification, 370.152 9 Intelligence, 370.153 2 Personality, and .153 4 Emotions have been added. The title of number 372.37 has been changed from Health (hygiene) to Personal health and safety. This number is further expanded. In main class 381 Internal commerce, some new numbers viz. 381.11 Shopping centers, .177 Online auctions, .186 Street fairs, and .347 Better business bureaus have been included in DDC 22.

Language: Numerous expansions have been made to the schedule of Grammar of standard forms of languages 415. Under this number the standard subdivision .01 Philosophy and theory has been expanded. The new numbers 415.5 to 415.7 have been included to cover the word classes and 415.9 has been included to cover the morphology. The title of number 419 has been changed from Structured verbal language other than spoken and written to Sign languages. The provision of adding Table 2 to this number has also been made under number .4-.9. The schedule of other Germanic languages has been extensively expanded. Under the Chinese languages 495.1, to cover the dialects of different geographic regions of China, a provision under .171-.178 has been made to add number following -51 in notation 511-518 from Table 2.

Science: A substantial update has also been introduced in 510 Mathematics. Certain relocations have been made in 518 Numerical analysis. In the main class mathematics, some new numbers viz. .322 3 Fuzzy sets, .326 Functions and relations.

.332 Partially ordered sets, .352 1 Recursive functions, and .36 Proof theory and constructive mathematics have been incorporated. The schedules of 512.2 Groups and group theory, 512.3 Fields, 512.4 Rings, 512.55 Topological and related algebras and groups have been expanded. A new number 512.6 with expansions .62, .64 & .66 to cover Category theory, Homological algebra, and K-theory have been included. Other numbers which have been revised /and expanded in mathematics are 515.39, 515.94, 516.15, 518, 519.236, and 519.6. In main class Astronomy and allied sciences, the title of 523.2 has been changed from Solar system to Planetary system and a new number .24 has been included for extrasolar systems. The number for Quantum electrodynamics has been relocated from 537.67 to 530.143 3. The numbers of zeros for the use of standard subdivisions with 543 have been reduced from two to one. The schedule of Analytical chemistry 543 has been totally revised. The use of numbers 544, 545 and 547.3 has been discontinued and these are relocated under 543. The number 560.4 has been expanded and new numbers .41 Fossilization, .43 Tracefossils, and .47 Micropaleontology have been included. In main class paleobotany, numbers 561.1 has been expanded to include the stratigraphic paleobotany. The other numbers revised /and expanded includes 569.9, 578.62, 579.17, 591.5, 597.8, and 597.9.

Technology: The schedule of Medicine and health 610 has been updated and expanded, and indexing for medical topics has been improved. In the main class 610 Medicine and health, use of the number 610.736 1 to .736 9 has been discontinued and relocated to other places. The numbers relocated in medicine from other places are 613.66 Self-defense, 613.663 Rape prevention for individuals, and 613.72 Massage. Numerous numbers in the schedule of medicine have been expanded, these include 611.018 16, 613.79, 614.1, 615.822, 617.919, 617.95, and 618.24. Several new numbers under 616 & 617 have also been incorporated. Two numbers 621.388 06 Highdefinition television (HDTV) and 621.388 07 Digital television have been included under the number 621.388 Television. As many as 27 new numbers have been included in the schedule of Food and drinks 641. A few new numbers have also been included in 643, 645, and 646. The new numbers which have been included in the schedule of Management and auxiliary services are 650.11 Time management, 650.142 Resumes, cover letters, job applications, 650.144 Employment interviewing, 651.791 Intranets, 658.041 2 Home-based business, 658.312 3 Telecommuting, 658.405 8 Contracting out, and 659.144 Advertising in digital media.

Arts & recreation: In the schedule of arts & recreation, the numbers 775-777 were unassigned after the edition 14 of DDC. In DDC 22, two of these numbers have been used. The number 775 is used for Digital photography and 776 for Computer art (Digital art). The other new numbers included in the schedule of arts & recreation are: 704.943 43 [Iconography of] flowers, 736.96 Sand sculpture, 745.514 Woodburning, 796.046 Extreme sports, 796.522 4 Sport climbing, 796.67 Street luge racing, and 796.939 Snowboarding.

Literature: In the main class literature, the schedules of the number 839.5, .6, and .7 of other Germanic languages have been revised and a new number 891.469 for Konkani literature has been included.

History & geography: The facilities for travelers has been moved from 647.94 to 910.46 and to specific area numbers in 913-919, and updated historical periods throughout 930-990 have been introduced.

A single look on the first summary of DDC 22 reflects several changes like: Computer science, information & general works have taken place of generalities; Natural sciences & mathematics has been changed with science; The arts Fine and decorative arts has been replaced by Arts & recreation; Literature has taken place of Literature & rhetoric. The author is of the view that the removal of Table 7 will certainly enhance the classifier's efficiency. The continuous revision policy of DDC has made it the most used classification scheme. The physical get up of DDC 22 is attractive and its availability in digital form i.e. on the web will make instant availability of the updates to the users of DDC. Now the updates of DDC are single mouse click ahead of the classifier.

3

INTRODUCTION TO THE SCHEDULES

After going through chapter 1, you are now able to make some simple class numbers. Let us start with examples of simple class numbers.

Electronic mail	**004.692**
Class No.	004.692
Word processing programs	**005.52**
Class No.	005.52
Administration of Library building	**022.3**
Class No.	022.3
Universal Decimal Classification	**025.432**
Class No.	025.432
Children library	**027.625**
Class No.	027.625
Furniture in Museums	**069.33**
Class No.	069.33
Radio Broadcast Media	**070.194**
Class No.	070.194

Psychology of young women	**155.533**
Class No.	155.533
Environmental psychology	**155.9**
Class No.	155.9
Vedanta Philosophy	**181.48**
Class No.	181.48
Hinduism	**294.5**
Class No.	294.5
Koran	**297.122**
Class No.	297.122
Political ideologies	**320.5**
Class No.	320.5
Democratic Government	**321.8**
Class No.	321.8
Political parties	**324.2**
Class No.	324.2
Constitution of labour unions	**331.871**
Class No.	331.871
Commercial banks	**332.12**
Class No.	332.12
Comparative law	**342.2**
Class No.	342.2

Income tax law	**343.052**
Class No.	343.052
Personal property law	**346.047**
Class No.	346.047
Personnel administration in Military	**355.61**
Class No.	355.61
Criminal offences	**364.1**
Class No.	364.1
Problems of discipline in schools	**371.58**
Class No.	371.58
Wholesale trade	**381.2**
Class No.	381.2
Linear algebra	**512.5**
Class No.	512.5
Differential topology	**514.72**
Class No.	514.72
Solid analytic geometry	**516.33**
Class No.	516.33
Jupiter planet	**523.45**
Class No.	523.45
Molecular Physics	**539.6**
Class No.	539.6

Stereochemistry	**541.223**
Class No.	541.223
Cell biology	**571.6**
Class No.	571.6
Biochemistry	**573.44**
Class No.	573.44
Animal Genetics	**591.35**
Class No.	591.35
Reptilia	**596.9**
Class No.	596.9
Homeopathy	**615.532**
Class No.	615.532
Disease of blood	**616.15**
Class No.	616.15
Heart surgery	**617.412**
Class No.	517.412
Magnetic engineering	**621.34**
Class No.	621.34
Artillery engineering	**623.41**
Class No.	623.41
Road-Repair Engineering	**625.761**
Class No.	625.761

Wheat crops	**633.11**
Class No.	633.11
Breeds of dogs	**636.71**
Class No.	636.71
Hunting birds	**639.12**
Class No.	639.12
Sandwich cooking	**641.84**
Class No.	641.84
Advanced accounting	**657.046**
Class No.	657.046
Recruitment and selection of personnel	**658.311**
Class No.	658.311
Cotton textile	**677.21**
Class No.	677.21
Nightclothes	**687.165**
Class No.	687.165
Air conditioning engineering	**697.93**
Class No.	697.93
Calligraphy	**745.61**
Class No.	745.61
Folk music	**781.62**
Class No.	781.62

Cricket	**796.358**
Class No.	796.358

History of India under Akbar	**954.025 4**
Class No.	954.025 4

20th century history of Kenya	**967.620 3**
Class No.	967.620 3

Class numbers can also be made by following the various notes. Many notes have been elaborated in chapter 1. Now we will make some class numbers by following the notes.

ASCII character set	**005.722**
Character set	005.722
Note : Including ASCII	
Class No.	005.722
(This is an including note)	

National Library	**027.5**
Government Library	027.5
Note : National, state, provincial, local	
Class No.	027.5
(This is a scope note)	

Foreign news	**070.433 2**
International news	070.433 2
Note : Class here foreign news	
Class No.	070.433 2
(This is a class here note)	

Sentiments	**152.4**
Emotions	152.4
Note : Class here affects, ... sentiments	
Class No.	152.4
(This is a class here note)	
Modern Eastern philosophy	**181**
Eastern philosophy	181
Note : Ancient, medieval, modern	
Class No.	181
(This is a scope note)	
Soteriology	**234**
Salvation and grace	234
Note : Variant name for salvation: soteriology	
Class No.	234
(This is a variant name note)	
Training of individual and units in military	**355.5**
Military training	355.5
Note : Training of individual and units	
Class No.	335.5
(This is a definition note)	
Soil biochemistry	**631.417**
Organic soil chemistry	631.417
Note : Class here soil biochemistry	
Class No.	631.417
(This is a class here note)	
Maize crops	**633.15**
Corn crops	633.15
Note : Variant names: Indian corn, maize	

Class No. 631.417

(This is a variant name note)

Plastics Pollution control technology **668.419 2**

Plastics waste technology 668.419 2

Note : Class here pollution control

Class No. 668.419 2

(This is a class here note)

These are the very simple notes. One note which I found a number of distance education students struggling with is an add note. If this note is taken as mathematical application, it is very simple to follow. In simple terms, an add note instruct the classifier to add certain number or part of this from a range specified in this note. Let's look the format of add note and its mathematical step-by-step application.

Suppose you have to classify a title "Law libraries".

You have to take the following steps and your class number is ready. You will find in third summary a number 026 Libraries, archives, information centers devoted to specific subjects and disciplines. In schedule, under its subdivisions you will find .001-.999 Specific subjects and disciplines and below this there is an add note which reads as under:

Add to base number 026 notation 001-999.

Follow the following steps:

Step 1. Note the base number 026

Step 2. Go to schedule and find a suitable number for Law from 000 to 999 .340

Step 3. Suffix this number to the base number 026+340

Step 4. Rewrite the number 026.34

(**Note:** Here a dot is inserted after first three digits and the last zero is omitted because it was there only to complete the minimum three digits.)

More examples with somewhat more difficult add note.

1. Title: Hindu Temples

294.5 is Hinduism and 294.51-.53 is Mythology, relations, doctrines, public worship and other practices and below to this is an add note.

Add to base number 294.5 the numbers following 20 in 201-203.

Follow the following steps:

Step 1. Note the base number 294.5

Step 2. Go to 201 to 203 in schedule and find a suitable number for Temples. 203.5

Step 3. Omit the number written between the words **"between"** and **"in"** in the note (e.g. 20 in this note) from the number obtained at step 2 ~~20~~3.5

Step 4. Add the remaining number to the base number 294.5+35

Step 5. Rewrite the number 294.535

2. Title: Raising of goats for Milk

636.39 is Goats and 636.391 is Goats for specific purposes and below to this is an add note.

Add to base number 636.391 the numbers following 636.088 in 636.0882-636.0889.

Follow the following steps:

Step 1. Note the base number 636.391

Step 2. Go to 636.0882 to 636.0889 in schedule and find a suitable number for Animals raised for eggs and milk 636.088 42

Step 3. Omit the number written between the words **"between"** and **"in"** in the note (e.g. 636.088 in this note) from the number obtained at step 2 ~~636.088~~ 42

Step 4. Add the remaining number to the base number 636.391+42

Step 5. Rewrite the number 636.391 42

In the next few pages the class numbers made according to above formula are provided.

Classification of Financial Economics **025.463 32**

Base Number	025.46
Instruction	Add to base number 025.46 notation 001-999
Financial Economics	332
	= 025.46+332
Class No.	025.463 32

Biochemistry Libraries **026.572**

Base Number	026
Instruction	Add to base number 026 notation 001-999
Biochemistry	572
	=026+572
Class No.	026.572

Tests for cricket umpiring ability **153.947 963 583**

Base Number	153.94
Instruction	Add to base number 153.94 notation 001-999
Cricket umpiring	796.358 3
	=153.94+796.358 3
Class No.	153.947 963 583

Development of self-control among children **155.418 25**

Base Number	155.418 2
Instruction	Add to base number 155.418 2 the numbers following 155.2 in 155.22-155.28
Development of self-control	~~155.2~~5
	=155.418 2+5
Class No.	155.418 25

Personal-social behavior of preschool children	**155.423 8**
Base Number	155.423
Instruction	Add to base number 155.423 the numbers following 155.41 in 155.412-418
Personal-social behavior	~~155.41~~8
	=155.423+8
Class No.	155.423 8

Intelligence test for school children	**155.424 393**
Base Number	155.424
Instruction	Add to base number 155.424 the numbers following 155.41 in 155.412-418
Conscious mental processes and intelligence	~~155.41~~3
Instruction	Add to base number 155.413 the numbers following 153 in 153.1-153.9

Base Number	~~155.41~~3
Intelligence test	~~153~~.93
	=~~155.41~~3+93
	=155.424+3+93
Class No.	155.424 393

Tests for mathematical ability among school children	**155.424 394 51**
Base Number	155.424
Instruction	Add to base number 155.424 the numbers following 155.41 in 155.412-418
Conscious mental processes and intelligence	~~155.41~~3
Instruction	Add to base number 155.413 the numbers following 153 in 153.1-153.9
Base Number	~~155.41~~3
Aptitude test	~~153~~.94
	=3+94
Instruction	Add to base number 153.94 notation 001-999
Base Number	~~153~~.94
Mathematics	510
	=~~153~~.94+510
	=155.424+3+94+510
Class No.	155.424 394 51

Ethics of marriage in Hinduism	**294.548 63**
Base Number	294.548 6

Instruction	Add to base number 294.5486 the numbers following 17 in 172-179
Ethics of marriage	~~17~~3
	=294.548 6+3
Class No.	294.548 63

Animal husbandry in Halakhah	**296.188 636**
Base Number	296.188
Instruction	Add to base number 296.188 notation 001-999
Animal husbandry	636
	=296.188 +636
Class No.	296.188 636

Commentaries on Hadith	**297.124 07**
Base Number	297.124 0
Instruction	Add to base number 297.124 0 the numbers following 297.122 in 297.1221-297.1228
Commentaries	~~297.122~~ 7
	=297.124 0+7
Class No.	297.124 07

Women pilots	**305.436 291 309 2**
Base Number	305.43
Instruction	Add to base number 305.43 notation 001-999
Pilots	629.130 92
	=305.43+629.130 92
Class No.	305.436 291 309 2

Industrial relations in Furniture occupations	**331.041 651 23**
Base Number	331.041
Instruction :	Add to base number 331.041 notation 001-999
Furniture occupations	651.23
	=331.041+651.23
Class No.	331.041 651 23

Mines as Military equipment	**355.825 115**
Base Number	355.82
Instruction	Add to base number 355.82 the numbers following 623.4 in 623.43-623.46
Mines	~~623.4~~51 15
	=355.82+5115
Class No.	355.825 115

Protective measures for thunderstorms	**363.349 247 2**
Base Number	363.349 2
Instruction	Add to base number 363.349 2 the numbers following 551.55 in 551.552-551.556; then add further as instructed under 362-363.
Thunderstorms	~~551.554~~
Protective measures (table under 362-363)	72
	=363.349 2+4+72
Class No.	363.349 247 2

Teacher-Parent relations in secondary schools **373.110 3**

Base Number 373.1

Instruction Add to base number 373.1 the numbers following 371 in 371.1-371.8

Teacher-Parent relations ~~371~~.103

=373.1+103

Class No. 373.110 3

Costumes of nobility **391.023**

Base Number 391.0

Instruction Add to base number 391.0 the numbers following 390 in 390.1-390.4

Nobility ~~390~~.23

=391.0+23

Class No. 391.023

Euclidean of three-dimensionall cubes **516.215 6**

Base Number 516.21

Instruction Add to base number 516.21 the numbers following 516.1 in 516.12-516.18

Three-dimensional cubes ~~516.1~~56

=516.21+56

Class No. 516.215 6

Astrophysics of heat radiation **523.013 3**

Base Number 523.013

Instruction Add to base number 523.013 the numbers

	following 536 in 536.1-536.7
Heat radiation	~~536.~~3
	=523.013+3
Class No.	523.013 3
Orbit of Pluto	**523.482 3**
Base Number (Pluto*)	523.482
Instruction	Add to notation for each number identified by * the numbers following 523.3 in 523.31-523.33
Orbit	~~523.3~~3
	=523.482+3
Class No.	523.482 3

(Note here instruction is provided as foot note with * mark)

Dimensions of Neptune satellites	**523.988 11**
Base Number	523.98
Instruction	Add to base number 523.98 the numbers following 523.4 in 523.43-523.48
Neptune*	523.481
Instruction	Add to notation for each number identified by * the numbers following 523.3 in 523.31-523.33
Dimensions	~~523.3~~1
	=523.98+81+1
Class No.	523.988 11

Sikh calendar	**529.324 6**
Base Number	529.32
Instruction	Add to base number 529.32 the numbers following 29 in 292-299
Sikhism	~~29~~4.6
	=529.32+46
Class No.	529.324 6

Magnetic properties of plasmas	**530.442**
Base Number	530.44
Instruction	Add to base number 530.44 the numbers following 530.41 in 530.412-530.416
Magnetic properties	~~530.41~~2
	=530.44+2
Class No.	530.442

Liquid-state chemistry	**541.042 2**
Base Number	541.042
Instruction	Add to base number 541.042 the numbers following 530.4 in 530.41-530.44
Liquid-state	~~530.4~~2
	=541.042+2
Class No.	541.042 2

Photochemistry of Hydrosulfides	**547.063 045 5**
Base Number (Hydrosulfides*)	547.063
Instruction	Add to each subdivision identified by * as follows:

Physical chemistry	045
Instruction	Add to base number 045 the numbers following 541.3 in 541.33-541.38
Photochemistry	~~541.3~~5
	=547.063+045+5
Class No.	547.063 045 5

Aliphatic alcoholic compounds	**547.431**
Base Number	547.4
Instruction	Add to base number 547.4 the numbers following 547.0 in 547.02-547.08
Alcoholic	~~547.0~~31
	=547.4+31
Class No.	547.431

Determinative mineralogy in Pyroclastic rocks	**549.114 23**
Base Number	549.114
Instruction	Add to base number 549.114 the numbers following 552 in 552.1-552.5
Pyroclastic rocks	~~552~~.23
	=549.114+23
Class No.	549.114 23

Variations in snow and snowfall over time	**551.578 43**
Base Number	551.578 4
Instruction	Add to base number 551.578 4 the numbers

following 551.577 in 551.5771-551.5773

Variations over time ~~551.577~~ 3

=551.578 4+3

Class No. 551.578 43

Mississippian paleontology **560.175 1**

Base Number 560.17

Instruction Add to base number 560.17 the numbers following 551.7 in 551.71-551.79

Mississippian ~~551.7~~51

=560.17+51

Class No. 560.175 1

Archeozoic paleobotany **561.111 2**

Base Number 561.11

Instruction Add to base number 561.11 the numbers following 551.7 in 551.71-551.79

Archeozoic ~~551.7~~12

=561.11+12

Class No. 561.111 2

Fossil Conjugales **561.933 7**

Base Number 561.93

Instruction Add to base number 561.93 the numbers following 579.8 in 579.82-579.89

Conjugales	~~579.8~~37
	=561.93+37
Class No.	561.933 7

Physiology of beetles	**571.157 6**
Base Number	571.1
Instruction	Add to base number 571.1 the numbers following 59 in 590.1-599
Beetles	~~59~~5.76
	=571.1+576
Class No.	571.157 6

Analytical biochemistry of Copper	**572.518 36**
Base Number (Copper†)	572.518
Instruction	Except for modification shown under specific entries, add to each subdivision identified by † as follows:
Anatomy and application of specific process to other processes	33-39
Instruction	Add to 3 the numbers following 572.3 in 572.33-572.39
Analytical biochemistry	~~572.36~~
	=572.518+3+6
Class No.	572.518 36

(**Note:** Here instruction is provided through footnote with † mark)

Organisms characteristic of forest	**578.73**

Base Number 578.7

Instruction Add to base number 578.7 the numbers following 577 in 577.3-577.5

Forest ~~577~~.3

=578.7+3

Class No. 578.73

Reproductive adaptation of Box lily **584.353 146**

Base Number (Box lily*) 584.353

Instruction Except for modification shown under specific entries, add to each subdivision identified by * as follows:

General topics of natural history of plants 1

Instruction Add to base number 1 the numbers following 581 in 581.3-581.7

Reproductive adaptation ~~581~~.46

=584.353+1+46

Class No. 584.353 146

Treatment of Hypertension by Radiotherapy **616.132 064 2**

Base Number (Hypertension*) 616.132

Instruction Except for modification shown under specific entries, add to each subdivision identified by * as follows:

Other therapies 062-069

Instruction	Add to 06 the numbers following 615.8 in 615.82-615.89
Radiotherapy	~~615.8~~42 =616.132+06+42
Class No.	616.132 064 2
Treatment of Typhoid by climatotherapy	**616.927 206 34**
Base Number (Typhoid *)	616.927 2
Instruction	Except for modification shown under specific entries, add to each subdivision identified by * as follows:
Other therapies	062-069
Instruction	Add to 06 the numbers following 615.8 in 615.82-615.89
Climatotherapy	~~615.8~~34 =616.927 2+06+34
Class No.	616.927 206 34
Laser Surgery of Cancer	**616.994 059 8**
Base Number (Cancer †)	616.994
Instruction	Except for modification shown under specific entries, add to each subdivision identified by † as follows:
Laser Surgery	059 8 =616.994 +059 8
Class No.	616.994 059 8

Drug therapy of Lung cancer	**616.994 240 61**
Base Number	616.994
Instruction	Add to base number 616.994 the numbers following 611 in 611.2-611.9 and then add further as instructed under 618.1-618.8
Lung	~~611~~.24
Drug therapy	061
	=616.994+24+061
Class No.	616.994 240 61

Intensive care for head surgery	**617.510 28**
Base Number (head*)	617.51
Instruction	Except for modification shown under specific entries, add to each subdivision identified by * as follows:
Intensive care	028
	=617.51+028
Class No.	617.510 28

Plastic surgery of Nose	**617.523 059 2**
Base Number (Nose *)	617.523
Instruction	Except for modification shown under specific entries, add to each subdivision identified by * as follows:
Plastic surgery	0592
	=617.523+059 2
Class No.	617.523 059 2

First aid for legs surgery	**617.584 026 2**
Base Number (legs *)	617.584
Instruction	Except for modification shown under specific entries, add to each subdivision identified by * as follows:
First aid	026 2
	=617.584+026 2
Class No.	617.584 026 2

Treatment of women disease by drug therapy	**618.106 2**
Base Number (Gynecology *)	618.1
Instruction	Except for modification shown under specific entries, add to each subdivision identified by * as follows:
Drug therapy	06 2
	=618.1+06 2
Class No.	618.106 2

Treatment of Tuberculosis among old age patients	**618.976 995 06**
Base Number	618.976
Instruction	Add to base number 618.976 the numbers following 616 in 616.1-616.9
Tuberculosis*	~~616~~.995
Instruction	Except for modification shown under specific

entries, add to each subdivision identified by * as follows:

Treatment 06

=618.976+995+06

Class No. 618.976 995 06

Diagnosis of smallpox among children **618.929 120 75**

Base Number 618.92

Instruction Add to base number 618.92 the numbers following 616 in 616.1-616.9

Smallpox * ~~616~~.912

Instruction Except for modification shown under specific entries, add to each subdivision identified by * as follows:

Diagnosis 075

=618.92+912+075

Class No. 618.929 120 75

Interior Lighting in National Library building **621.322 782 5**

Base Number 621.322

Instruction Add to base number 621.322 the numbers following 72 in 725-728

Library building ~~72~~7.82

Instruction Add to base number ~~72~~7.82 the numbers

	following 027 in 027.1-027.8
National Library	~~027~~.5
	=621.322+782+5
Class No.	621.322 782 5
Piloting of Commercial airplanes	**629.132 524 042 3**
Base Number	629.132 52
Instruction	Add to base number 629.132 52 the numbers following 629.133 3 in 629.133 33-629.133 38
Commercial airplanes	~~629.133 3~~40 423
	=629.132 52+404 23
Class No.	629.132 524 042 3
Dry farming of wheat	**633.118 6**
Base Number (wheat*)	633.11
Instruction	Except for modification shown under specific entries, add to each subdivision identified by * as follows:
Special cultivation methods	8
Instruction	Add to 8 the numbers following 631.58 in 631.581-631.587
Dry farming	~~631.58~~6
	= 633.11+8+6
Class No.	633.118 6

Ammonium nitrate fertilizer for Lime crops	**634.337 894 2**
Base Number (Limes *)	634.337
Instruction	Except for modification shown under specific entries, add to each subdivision identified by * as follows:
Fertilizers, soil conditions, growth regulators	89
Instruction	Add to 89 the numbers following 631.8 in 631.81-631.89
Ammonium nitrate fertilizer	~~631.8~~42
	=634.337+89+42
Class No.	634.337 894 2

Control of Scorpion flies in watermelons crops	**635.615 974 4**
Base Number (watermelons*)	635.615
Instruction	Except for modification shown under specific entries, add to each subdivision identified by * as follows:
Injuries, disease, pests	9
Instruction	Add to 9 the numbers following 632 in 632.1-632.9
Insect pests	~~632~~.7
Instruction	Add to base number ~~632~~.7 the numbers following 595.7 in 595.72-595.79

Scorpion flies ~~595.7~~44
=635.615+9+7+44

Class No. 635.615 974 4

Grafting of flowering plants **635.915 41**

Base Number 635.91

Instruction Add to base number 635.91 the numbers following 631 in 631.2-631.8

Grafting ~~631~~.541
=635.91+541

Class No. 635.915 41

Artificial insemination of Horses **636.108 245**

Base Number 636.10

Instruction Add to base number 636.10 the numbers following 636.0 in 636.001-636.08

Artificial insemination ~~636.0~~82 45
=636.10+824 5

Class No. 636.108 245

Green fodder for Cattle **636.208 6**

Base Number 636.20

Instruction Add to base number 636.20 the numbers following 636.0 in 636.001-636.08

Green fodder ~~636.0~~86
=636.20+86

Class No. 636.208 6

Treatment of Bacterial disease in Dogs	**636.708 969 206**
Base Number	636.70
Instruction	Add to base number 636.70 the numbers following 636.0 in 636.001-636.08
Veterinary medicine	~~636.0~~89
Instruction	Add to base number 636.089 the numbers following 61 in 610-618
Bacterial disease*	~~61~~6.92
Instruction	Except for modification shown under specific entries, add to each subdivision identified by * as follows:
Treatment	06
	=636.70+89+692+06
Class No.	636.708 969 206

Child rearing for Adopted children	**649.145**
Base Number	649.14
Instruction	Add to base number 649.14 the numbers following 155.44 in 155.442-155.446
Adopted children	~~155.44~~5
	=649.14+5
Class No.	649.145

Spinning of Cotton for textiles	**677.212 2**
Base Number	677.21

Instruction	Add to base number 677.21 the numbers following 677.028 in 677.0282-677.0287
Spinning	~~677.028~~ 22
	=677.21+22
Class No.	677.212 2

Building for Mahabharata Museum	**727.629 459 23**
Base Number	727.6
Instruction	Add to base number 727.6 notation 001-999
Mahabharata	294.592 3
	=727.6+294.592 3
Class No.	727.629 459 23

Expressionism in sculpture	**735.230 442**
Base Number	735.230 4
Instruction	Add to base number 735.230 4 the numbers following 709.040 in 709.0401-709.0407
Expressionism	~~709.040~~ 42
	=735.230 4+42
Class No.	735.230 442

Paintings of Hindu Gods	**758.929 452 11**
Base Number	758.9
Instruction	Add to base number 758.9 notation 001-999
Hinduism	294.5
Instruction	Add to base number 294.5

	the numbers following 20 in 201-203
Gods	~~20~~2.11
	=758.9+294.5+211
Class No.	758.929 452 11

Arrangement of bass flutes in Jainism sacred music	**781.744 388 34**
Base Number	781.7
Instruction	Add to base number 781.7 the numbers following 29 in 294-299; then add further as follows:
Jainism	~~29~~4.4
Instruction	Add to base number 0 the numbers following 781 in 781.1-781.6
Arrangement	~~781~~.38
Instruction	Add to base number ~~781~~.38 the numbers following 78 in 782-788
Bass flutes	~~78~~8.34
	=781.7+44+38+834
Class No.	781.744 388 34

Leopard hunting as a game	**799.259 755 4**
Base Number	799.25
Instruction	Add to base number 799.25 the numbers following 59 in 592-599
Leopard	~~59~~9.755 4
	=799.25+975 54
Class No.	799.259 755 4

WORKS OF LAW

In the preceding pages we have dealt with all the schedules except 400-499, 340-349, 800-899 and 900-999. The schedule of languages i.e. 400-499 is dealt in chapter 7 and schedule of literature i.e. 800-899 is dealt in chapter six. The schedules of law 340-349 and 900-999 are being dealt in the next few pages. There is a definite reason for dealing with these schedules separately. The reason is the procedure of making class number from these schedules is little bit different. Let us try it.

The class numbers of Works of law in DDC are made under 340 and its subdivisions. The works of law can be divided into two categories.

1. Works on International law
2. Works on law other than international law

The works on/and about international law are to be classified under 341. In this category class numbers can be made of treaties, disputes and conflicts among countries, war, etc. Let us take first of all some examples of International law.

Indian treaties	**341.026 454**
Base Number	341.026 4
Instruction	Add to base number 341.026 4 notation 1-9 from Table 2
India (Table 2)	-54
	=341.026 4+54
Class No.	341.026 454

Treaties between China and Japan	**341.026 651 052**
Base Number	341.026 6
Instruction	Add to base number 341.026 6 notation 3-9

	from Table 2; then add 0 and again add notation 3-9 from Table 2.
China (Table 2)	-51
Indicator digit	0
Japan (Table 2)	-52
	=341.026 6+51+0+52
Class No.	341.026 651 052

Extraterrestrial space Treaties between Germany and New Zealand	**341.470 266 430 93**
Base Number (Extraterrestrial space†)	341.47
Instruction	Except for modification shown under specific entries, add to each subdivision identified by † as follows:
Text of treaties	0261-0266
Instruction	Add to base number 026 the numbers following 341.026 in 341.0261-341.0266
Bilateral treaties	~~341.026~~ 6
Instruction	Add to base number ~~341.026~~ 6 notation 3-9 from Table 2; then add 0 and again add notation 3-9 from Table 2.
Germany (Table 2)	-43
Indicator digit	0
New Zealand (Table 2)	-93
	=341.47+026+6+43+0+93
Class No.	341.470 266 430 93

Disarmament Treaties between UK and USA	**341.733 026 641 073**
Base Number (Disarmament†)	341.733
Instruction	Except for modification shown under specific entries, add to each subdivision identified by † as follows:
Text of treaties	0261-0266
Instruction	Add to base number 026 the numbers following 341.026 in 341.0261-341.0266
Bilateral treaties	~~341.026~~ 6
Instruction	Add to base number ~~341.026~~ 6 notation 3-9 from Table 2; then add 0 and again add notation 3-9 from Table 2.
UK (Table 2)	-41
Indicator digit	0
USA (Table 2)	-73
	=341.733+026+6+41+0+73
Class No.	341.733 026 641 073

Class numbers for law of specific jurisdictions and areas may be built from following five elements:

1. The base number that is indicating law 34
2. A digit indicating specific branch of law, original materials, or comprehensive works as follows:

   Constitutional and administrative law 2

   Military, defense, public property, public finance, tax, trade, industrial law 3

Labour, social service, education, cultural law	4
Criminal law	5
Private law	6
Civil procedure and courts	7
Laws (statutes), regulations, cases not limited to a specific branch	8
Comprehensive works	9

3. The facet indicator — 0
4. One or more digits indicating a subject subordinate to specific branch of law or type of original material

For example: Courts	1
Trials	7

5. Notation from Table 2 indicating the jurisdiction or area

For example: India	-54

To show comprehensive works on a specific jurisdiction or area in modern world, the elements are to be arranged as under:

1. Base number
2. Digit indicating comprehensive works
3. Jurisdiction or area

For example:

Law of India	**349.54**
Base Number	34
Comprehensive works	9
India (Table 2)	-54
	=34+9+54
Class No.	349.54

To show a specific branch, a specific subject, or a kind of original material, arrange the elements as follows:

1. Base number
2. Branch of law
3. Jurisdiction or area
4. Facet indicator (0)
5. Subordinate subject in branch of law

For example:

Income-tax law of India	**343.540 52**
Base Number	34
Branch of law	3
India (Table 2)	-54
Facet indicator	0
Income tax	52
	=34+3+54+0+52
Class No.	343.540 52

Generally this is the way of classifying works on law other than international law. However, there are three other preferred optional procedures, which are explained below. The examples in this book have been solved according to above procedure.

Option 1. To give local emphasis and a shorter notation to law of a specific jurisdiction or area, the elements can be arranged as under:

1. Base number
2. Branch of law
3. Facet indicator (0)
4. Subordinate subject in the branch of law

(For law of a jurisdiction subordinate to the emphasized jurisdiction or area, insert between the branch of law and facet indicator the notation indicating the subordinate jurisdiction)

The above class number will be like this:

Income tax law of India	**343.052**
Base Number	34
Branch of law	3
Facet indicator	0
Income tax	52
	=34+3+0+52
Class No.	343.052

(Please note here to show subordinate jurisdiction of an area with regular notation from Table 2, derive the notation by dropping from the area number for subordinate jurisdiction all digits that apply to preferred jurisdiction. For example, drop area number for India -54 from area number for Haryana -545 58 to obtain notation 558, which is to be used for Haryana. Thus the class number for Income tax law in Haryana is 343.558 052.

Option 2. To give preferred treatment to jurisdictions in general, arrange elements as follows:

1. Base number
2. Jurisdiction or area
3. Facet indicator (0)
4. Branch of law
5. Subordinate subject in the branch of law

The same class number will be like this:

Income tax law of India	**345.403 52**
Base Number	34
India (Table 2)	54
Facet indicator	0
Branch of law	3
Income tax	52
	=34+54+0+3+52
Class No.	345.403 52

Option 3. To give preferred treatment to branch of law and its subordinate subjects, the elements can also be arranged as follows:

1. Base number
2. Branch of law
3. Subordinate subject in the branch of law
4. Facet indicator (0)
5. Jurisdiction or area

The above class number will become like this now:

Income tax law of India	**343.520 54**
Base Number	34
Branch of law	3
Income tax	52
Facet indicator	0
India (Table 2)	54
	=34+3+52+0+54
Class No.	343.520 54

In this way any document on law (other than Internationa law) may have four different class numbers according to the same edition of DDC. Hence classifier has to decide as to which of the above procedures is suitable for his/her library. However, students can assign class numbers to the titles in the examination according to any of the above four procedures. In this book the very firs procedure has been followed. Let us look other class numbers o law other than international law.

Legislative law of Italy	**342.450**
Base Number	3
Branch of law	
Itly (Table 2)	

Facet indicator	0
Legislative	5
	=34+2+45+0+5
Class No.	342.450 5

Court decisions on absentee voting in Sudan **342.624 072 026 43**

Base Number	34
Branch of law	2
Sudan (Table 2)	624
Facet indicator	0
Absentee voting*	72
Instruction	Except for modification shown under specific entries, add to each subdivision identified by * as follows:
Court decisions	026 43
	=34+2+624+0+72+026 43
Class No.	342.624 072 026 43

Cases of fiscal policy in Brazil **343.810 340 264**

Base Number	34
Branch of law	3
Brazil (Table 2)	81
Facet indicator	0
Fiscal policy*	34
Instruction	Except for modification shown under specific entries, add to each

subdivision identified by * as follows:

Cases	026 4
	=34+3+81+0+34+026 4
Class No.	343.810 340 264

Codes of Sales taxes law in Iran **343.550 552 026 32**

Base Number	34
Branch of law	3
Iran (Table 2)	55
Facet indicator	0
Sales tax law	552
Instruction	Except for modification shown under specific entries, add to each subdivision identified by * as follows:
Court codes	026 32
	=34+3+55+0+552+026 32
Class No.	343.550 552 026 32

Advisory opinions of attorney-general regarding migrant labour law in Canada **344.710 154 402 65**

Base Number	34
Branch of law	4
Canada (Table 2)	71
Facet indicator	0
Labour *	1
Instruction	Add to base number 344.01 the numbers following 331 in 331.1-

Migrant labour	~~331~~.544
Instruction	Except for modification shown under specific entries, add to each subdivision identified by * as follows:
Advisory opinions of attorney-general	026 5
	=34+4+71+0+1+544+026 5
Class No.	344.710 154 402 65

Administrative regulations for Cocaine abusers in Algeria **344.650 446 802 636**

Base Number	34
Branch of law	4
Algeria (Table 2)	65
Facet indicator	0
Services to substance users*	446
Instruction	Add to base number 344.0446 the numbers following 362.29 in 362.293-362.299
Cocaine	~~362.29~~8
Instruction	Except for modification shown under specific entries, add to each subdivision identified by * as follows:
Administrative regulations	026 36
	=34+4+65+0+446+8+026 36
Class No.	344.650 446 802 636

Statements of witnesses in assassination in Peru	**345.850 252 402 62**
Base Number	34
Branch of law	5
Peru (Table 2)	85
Facet indicator	0
Crimes *	2
Instruction	Add to base number 345.02 the numbers following 364.1 in 364.13-364.18
Assassination	~~364.1~~52 4
Instruction	Except for modification shown under specific entries, add to each subdivision identified by * as follows:
Statements of witnesses	026 2
	=34+5+85+0+2+524+026 2
Class No.	345.850 252 402 62

Digest of Divorce law in Russia	**346.470 166 026 48**
Base Number	34
Branch of law	6
Russia (Table 2)	47
Facet indicator	0
Divorce *	166
Instruction	Except for modification shown under specific entries, add to each subdivision identified by * as follows:

Digest	026 48
	=34+6+47+0+166+026 48
Class No.	346.470 166 026 48

Judges of Supreme courts in Bulgaria	**347.499 035 34**
Base Number	34
Branch of law	7
Bulgaria (Table 2)	499
Facet indicator	0
Supreme courts †	35
Instruction	Add to each subdivision identified by † as follows:
Judges	34
	=34+7+499+0+35-34
Class No.	347.499 03534

WORKS OF GENERAL HISTORY, GEOGRAPHY AND BIOGRAPHY

The term "General History" is used here intentionally because the historical and geographical treatment of specific discipline or subject should be classified under the discipline or subject concerned. For example: history of Libraries, in Library science; Social history, in Social science; Economic history, in Economics; etc. In the very beginning of the schedule of Hisory there is an instruction in this regard. The instruction reads as:

"Class historical and geographical treatment of a specific discipline or subject with the discipline or subject, plus notation 09 from Table 1, e.g. historical and geographic treatment of natural sciences 509, of economic situations and conditions 330.9, of purely political situations and conditions 320.9, history of military science 355.009."

The notation 900.1-9 is used for standard subdivisions of history and geography whereas 901 to 908 is used for standard subdivisions of history and 909 is devoted to World history. Hence General history of the world is to be classified under 909. Under 909 there is a special provision of making class numbers of history of ethnic and national groups. Let us try some examples:

16th Century World History	**909.5**
Class No.	909.5

20th Century World History	**909.825**
Class No.	909.825

World History of Marathas	**909.049 48**
Base Number	909.04
Instruction	Add to base number 909.04 notation 05-9 from Table 5
Marathas (Table 5)	-948
	=909.04+948
Class No.	909.049 48

World History of Tibetans in 17th century	**909.049 540 6**
Base Number	909.04
Instruction	Add to base number 909.04 notation 05-9 from Table 5; then add 0 and to the result add the numbers following 909 in 909.1-909.8
Tibetans (Table 5)	-954

17th century ~~909~~.6

=909.04+954+0+6

Class No. 909.049 540 6

(**Note:** Here one zero is added after 954 as per instruction given under 909.04)

World History of Punjabis in 13th Century **909.049 143 02**

Base Number 909.04

Instruction Add to base number 909.04 notation 05-9 from Table 5; then add 0 and to the result add the numbers following 909 in 909.1-909.8

Punjabis (Table 5) -914 3

13th century ~~909~~.2

=909.04+914 3+0+2

Class No. 909.049 143 02

The schedule of 910 to 919 is devoted to Geography and travel. The works of geography of any specific continents, countries, localities in modern world can be classified under 913 to 919. There is an instruction below 913-919 to this effect. The instruction is as under:

Add to base number 91 notation 3-9 from Table 2 and then add further as follows.

Examples are provided below:

Geography of Punjab **915.455 2**

Base Number 91

Instruction Add to base number 91 notation 3-9 from Table 2

Punjab (Table 2) -545 52

=91+545 52

Class No. 915.455 2

Physical Geography of Switzerland **914.940 2**

Base Number 91

Instruction Add to base number 91 notation 3-9 from Table 2

Switzerland (Table 2) -494

Physical Geography 02

=91+494+02

Class No. 914.940 2

(Notation 02 is taken from table under 913-919)

Travel in Sweden in 18th century **914.850 436**

Base Number 91

Instruction Add to base number 91 notation 3-9 from Table 2

Sweden (Table 2) -485

Travel 04

Instruction Add to 04 the historical period numbers following 0 that appear in subdivisions of 930-990

18th century .~~50~~36

=91+485+04+36

Class No. 914.850 436

Facilities for Travelers in India in Shahjahan's reign **915.406 125 7**

Base Number 91

Instruction	Add to base number 91 notation 3-9 from Table 2
India (Table 2)	-54
Facilities for Travelers	061
Instruction	Add to 061 the historical period numbers following 0 that appear in subdivisions of 930-990
Shahjahan's reign	.0257
	=91+54+061+257
Class No.	915.406 125 7

The schedule of 920 to 929 is devoted to Biography, genealogy, insignia but only 920 and 929 are used for General Biography and genealogy, names, insignia respectively. The rest numbers 921-928 are the optional numbers. There is a specific instruction right at the beginning of 920. The instruction is as under:

Class biography of persons associated with a specific discipline or subject with the discipline or subject, plus notation 092 from Table 1.

For example:

Biography of Dr. S R Ranganathan		**020.92**
Base Number		020
Instruction	020.1-9 subdivisions	Standard
Biography (Table 1)		-092
		=02+092
Class No.		020.92

However, DDC 22 provides three other options for classifying the works of biographies. These are:

Option A: Use subdivisions identified by *

Under this provision the numbers from 921 to 928 have been provided for the biographies of specific disciplines or subjects. These numbers have been shown as optional numbers by footnote. The major drawback of this option is the separation of works of biographies from other documents on the same subject. The use of biographies of a given subject is much expected by the users of that subject.

Option B: Class individual biography in 92 or B; class collected biography in 92 or 920 undivided.

Use of this option also invite the same drawback .

Option C: Class individual biography of men in 920.71; Class individual biography of women in 920.72.

(Prefer specific discipline or subject, plus notation 092 from Table 1.)

Therefore, all the works of biography of persons relating to a subject should be classified under that subject by using notation 092 from Table 1. Only general biographies should be classified under 920. Some examples are given below:

Biography of 16th century persons	**920.009 031**
Base Number	920.009 0
Instruction	Add to base number 920.0090 the numbers following -090 in notation 090 1-090 5 from Table 1
16th Century (Table 1)	-~~090~~ 31
	=920.009 0+31
Class No.	920.009 031

Biography of rural persons	**920.009 173 4**
Base Number	920.009 1
Instruction	Add to base number

	920.0091 the numbers following -1 in notation 11-19 from Table 2
Rural (Table 2)	-173 4
	=920.009 1+734
Class No.	920.009 173 4

Biography of Mongols	**920.009 294 2**
Base Number	920.0092
Instruction	Add to base number 920.009 2 notation 05-9 from Table 5
Mongols (Table 5)	-942
	=920.009 2+942
Class No.	920.009 294 2

Biography of persons resident in India	**920.054**
Base Number	920.0
Instruction	Add to base number 920.0 notation 3-9 from Table 2
India (Table 2)	-54
	=920.0+54
Class No.	920.054

The schedule from 930 to 999 is devoted to History of Ancient world; of specific continents, countries, localities; of extraterrestrial worlds. An add note is given at 930-990 to make the class number of works of General history. The note reads as under :

Add to base number 9 notation 3-9 from Table 2.

The examples are illustrated in the next few pages.

History of India during Aurangzeb	**954.025 8**
Base Number	9

Instruction	Add to base number 9 notation 3-9 from Table 2; then add further as follows:
India (Table 2)	-54
Historical periods	01-09
Instruction	Add to 0 the period division numbers following 0 from the appropriate continent, country, locality in 930-990
Aurangzeb Period	.~~0~~258
	=9+54+0+258
Class No.	954.025 8

Nineteenth Century Japanese History **952.025**

Base Number	9
Instruction	Add to base number 9 notation 3-9 from Table 2; then add further as follows:
Japan (Table 2)	-52
Historical periods	01-09
Instruction	Add to 0 the period division numbers following 0 from the appropriate continent, country, locality in 930-990
19th Century	.~~0~~25
	=9+52+0+25
Class No.	952.025

History of freedom struggle of Peru	**985.04**
Base Number	9
Instruction	Add to base number 9 notation 3-9 from Table 2; then add further as follows:
Peru (Table 2)	-85
Historical periods	01-09
Instruction	Add to 0 the period division numbers following 0 from the appropriate continent, country, locality in 930-990
Struggle for independence	-04
	=9+85+0+4
Class No.	985.04

Twentieth Century History of Switzerland	**949.407 3**
Base Number	9
Instruction	Add to base number 9 notation 3-9 from Table 2; then add further as follows:
Switzerland (Table 2)	-494
Historical periods	01-09
Instruction	Add to 0 the period division numbers following 0 from the appropriate continent, country, locality in 930-990

20th Century -4073

=9+494+0+73

Class No. 949.407 3

All these numbers can be assigned directly from the schedule also, but the procedure is same. However, the numbers for history of U S is an exception and the notation for period of history is added directly without a zero. The reason is very simple that the numbers for states of Unites states have been dealt separately in 974-979. The zero divisions have been used for standard subdivisions. For example:

Colonial period History of United States 973.2

Base Number 9

Instruction: Add to base number 9 notation 3-9 from Table 2; then add further as follows:

Switzerland (Table 2) -73

Colonial period .2

=9+73+2

Class No. 973.2

Let us now try some examples of class numbers of various states of countries other than United States.

History of Punjab during 19th century 954.552 031

Base Number 9

Instruction: Add to base number 9 notation 3-9 from Table 2; then add further as follows:

Punjab (Table 2) -545 52

Historical periods 01-09

Instruction	Add to 0 the period division numbers following 0 from the appropriate continent, country, locality in 930-990
19th Century	-031
	=9+545 52+0+31
Class No.	954.552 031

History of Orissa during 7th century **954.133 021**

Base Number	9
Instruction	Add to base number 9 notation 3-9 from Table 2; then add further as follows:
Orissa (Table 2)	-541 33
Historical periods	01-09
Instruction	Add to 0 the period division numbers following 0 from the appropriate continent, country, locality in 930-990
7th Century	-021
	=9+541 33+0+21
Class No.	954.133 021

History of Tamil Nadu during 17th century **954.820 258**

Base Number	9
Instruction	Add to base number 9 notation 3-9 from Table 2:

then add further as follows:

Tamil Nadu (Table 2) -548 2

Historical periods 01-09

Instruction — Add to 0 the period division numbers following 0 from the appropriate continent, country, locality in 930-990

17th Century .~~0~~258

=9+548 2+0+258

Class No. 954.820 258

History of Delhi under Mogul empire **954.560 25**

Base Number 9

Instruction — Add to base number 9 notation 3-9 from Table 2; then add further as follows:

Delhi (Table 2) -545 6

Historical periods 01-09

Instruction — Add to 0 the period division numbers following 0 from the appropriate continent, country, locality in 930-990

Mogul empire .~~0~~25

=9+545 6+0+25

Class No. 954.560 25

History of Baluchistan under Mohammad Ayub Khan **954.915 045**

Base Number	9
Instruction	Add to base number 9 notation 3-9 from Table 2; then add further as follows:
Baluchistan (Table 2)	-549 15
Historical periods	01-09
Instruction	Add to 0 the period division numbers following 0 from the appropriate continent, country, locality in 930-990
Administration of Mohammad Ayub Khan	.045 =9+549 915+0+45
Class No.	954.915 045

History of Edo state during Nigerian Civil war **966.932 052**

Base Number	9
Instruction	Add to base number 9 notation 3-9 from Table 2; then add further as follows:
Edo state (Table 2)	-669 32
Historical periods	01-09
Instruction	Add to 0 the period division numbers following 0 from the appropriate continent, country, locality in 930-990

Period of Nigerian Civil war .~~0~~52

=9+669 31+0+52

Class No. 966.932 052

History of Queensland during 1976-1983 **994.306 3**

Base Number 9

Instruction Add to base number 9 notation 3-9 from Table 2; then add further as follows:

Queensland (Table 2) -943

Historical periods 01-09

Instruction Add to 0 the period division numbers following 0 from the appropriate continent, country, locality in 930-990

1976-1983 .~~0~~63

=9+943+0+63

Class No. 994.306 3

History of Salamanca under Juan Carlos-I **946.250 83**

Base Number 9

Instruction Add to base number 9 notation 3-9 from Table 2; then add further as follows:

Salamanca (Table 2) -462 5

Historical periods 01-09

Instruction	Add to 0 the period division numbers following 0 from the appropriate continent, country, locality in 930-990
Reign of Juan Carlos-I	-083
	=9+462 5+0+83
Class No.	946.250 83

History of Alessandria under Napoleon	**945.140 82**
Base Number	9
Instruction	Add to base number 9 notation 3-9 from Table 2; then add further as follows:
Alessandria (Table 2)	-451 4
Historical periods	01-09
Instruction	Add to 0 the period division numbers following 0 from the appropriate continent, country, locality in 930-990
Napoleonic period	-082
	=9+451 4+0+82
Class No.	945.140 82

History of West Sussex under Elizabeth-I	**942.260 55**
Base Number	9

Instruction	Add to base number 9 notation 3-9 from Table 2; then add further as follows:
West Sussex (Table 2)	-422 6
Historical periods	01-09
Instruction	Add to 0 the period division numbers following 0 from the appropriate continent, country, locality in 930-990
Elizabeth-I	.055
	=9+422 6+0+55
Class No.	942.260 55

4
USE OF TABLE 1: STANDARD SUBDIVISIONS

As mentioned in the chapter1, 6 tables have been provided in DDC 22. The first table contains standard subdivisions. A standard subdivision represents a recurring physical form (such as an encyclopaedia, periodical, or index) or approach (such as history or research) and thus is applicable to any subject or discipline that covers or approximates the whole of the meaning of the number. These standard subdivisions are like common isolates in colon classification although these are not hundred percent same. The provision of standard subdivisions was made in the second edition of DDC published in 1885 for the first time and since then these have been called differently in different editions of DDC. The various names used for standard subdivisions are mention in the below table:

Sr. No.	Edition/s	Name used for standard subdivisions
1	2nd to 12th	Form Divisions
2	13th	Common Subdivisions
3	14th	Uniform Subdivisions
4	15th & 16th	Form Divisions
5	17th to 22nd	Standard Subdivisions

RULES FOR ADDING STANDARD SUBDIVISIONS

A standard subdivision (ss) is never used alone, but may

be used as required with any regular schedule number, e.g. Dictionary (-03 notation in Table 1) of Political science (320): 320.03. While adding the ss from Table 1 following rules must be followed.

Standard subdivisions can be added to any number in the schedule (without waiting for invitation to add ss) unless there is a specific instruction to the contrary. For example:

Encyclopaedia of Jainism	**294.403**
Jainism	294.4
Encyclopaedia (Table 1)	-03 (ss)
	= 294.4+03
Class No.	294.403

(Please note that the number for Jainism is 294.4 in the schedule and notation for encyclopaedia (-03) is provided in Table 1. We added a standard subdivision without waiting for an invitation or instruction to add standard subdivision.)

The most important caveat with respect to standard subdivisions is that they are added only for works that cover or approximate the whole of the subject of the number. For example, a work on black widow spiders of California should be classed in the number for spiders 595.44 (not 595.4409794). Here California should not be specified because black widow spiders do not approximate the whole universe of spiders in California, and there is not a specific number available for black widows.

If the ultimate class number is a main class or a division i.e. ends with one zero or two zeroes, the zeroes filling the vacant space are to be removed before adding a standard subdivision; and the digits are reshuffled so that the dot is put after the first three digits. For example:

Encyclopaedia of Philosophy	**103**
Philosophy	100

Encyclopaedia (Table 1)	-03 (ss)
	= 1~~00~~+03
Class No.	103

Periodicals of natural sciences	**505**
Natural sciences	500
Periodicals (Table 1)	-05 (ss)
	= 5~~00~~+05
Class No.	505

Philosophy and theory of Mathematics	**510.1**
Mathematics	51~~0~~
Philosophy and theory (Table 1)	-01 (ss)
	= 51~~0~~+01
Class No.	510.1

Use of standard subdivisions with one zero

If there is no indication of adding more than one zero, standard subdivisions may be used with one zero. Some examples of adding standard subdivisions with one zero are provided in the next few pages.

Philosophy of Library administration	**025.101**
Library administration	025.1
Philosophy (Table 1)	-01 (ss)
	= 025.1+01
Class No.	025.101

Classification of snakes	**597.960 12**
Snakes	597.96
Classification (Table 1)	-012 (ss)
	=597.96+012
Class No.	597.960 12

Language and communication in Inter Library Loan	**025.620 14**
Inter Library Loan	025.62
Language and communication (Table 1)	-014 (ss)
	= 025.62+014
Class No.	025.620 14

Acronyms in Vedanta philosophy	**181.480 148**
Vedanta philosophy	181.48
Acronyms (Table 1)	-014 8 (ss)
	= 181.48+014 8
Class No.	181.480 148

Scientific principles for Gold Technology	**669.220 15**
Gold Technology	669.22
Scientific principles (Table 1)	-015 (ss)
	= 669.22+0715
Class No.	669.220 15

Outline of Colon Classification	**025.435 020 2**
Colon Classification	025.435
Outline (Table 1)	-020 2 (ss)
	= 025.435+020 2
Class No.	025.435 020 2

Statistics of Boxing	**796.830 21**
Boxing	796.83
Statistics (Table 1)	-021 (ss)
	= 796.83+0 21
Class No.	796.830 21

Standards for software engineering	**005.102 18**
Software engineering	005.1

Standards (Table 1)	-021 8 (ss)
	= 005.1+021 8
Class No.	005.102 18

Use of Drawings in Secondary education	**373.022 2**
Secondary education	373
Drawings (Table 1)	-022 2 (ss)
	= 373+022 2
Class No.	373.022 2

Journalism as a profession	**070.402 3**
Journalism	070.4
Subject as a profession (Table 1)	-023 (ss)
	= 070.4+023
Class No.	070.402 3

Directory of Cooperative Societies	**334.702 5**
Cooperative Societies	334.7
Directory (Table 1)	-025 (ss)
	= 334.7+025
Class No.	334.702 5

Patents on Rice	**633.180 272**
Rice	633.18
Patents (Table 1)	-027 2 (ss)
	= 633.18+027 2
Class No.	633.180 272

Ownership marks of Washing machines	**683.880 277**
Washing machines	683.88
Ownership marks (Table 1)	-027 7 (ss)
	= 683.88+027 7
Class No.	683.880 277

Techniques of Leather Bookbinding	**686.342 028**
Leather Bookbinding	686.342
Techniques (Table 1)	-028 (ss)
	= 686.342+028
Class No.	686.342 028

Equipments for Cryptography	**652.802 84**
Cryptography	652.8
Equipments (Table 1)	-0284 (ss)
	= 652.8+028 4
Class No.	652.802 84

Computer Applications to Public libraries	**027.402 85**
Public libraries	027.4
Computer Applications (Table 1)	-028 5 (ss)
	= 027.4+028 5
Class No.	027.402 85

Dictionary of Child Psychology	**155.403**
Child Psychology	155.4
Dictionary (Table 1)	-03 (ss)
	= 155.4+03
Class No.	155.403

Encyclopaedia of Political Science	**320.03**
Political Science	320
Encyclopaedia (Table 1)	-03 (ss)
	=320+03
Class No.	320.03

Thesaurus of Law	**340.03**
Law	340
Thesaurus (Table 1)	-03 (ss)

	=340+03
Class No.	340.03

Periodicals on Comparative Psychology	**156.05**
Comparative Psychology	156
Periodicals (Table 1)	-05 (ss)
	=156+05
Class No.	156.05

Management of Political parties	**324.206 8**
Political parties	327.2
Management (Table 1)	-068 (ss)
	=327.2+068
Class No.	327.206 8

Personnel management of Central Banks	**332.110 683**
Central Banks	332.11
Personnel management (Table 1)	-068 3 (ss)
	=332.11+068 3
Class No.	332.110 683

Study of Astrology	**133.607**
Astrology	133.6
Study (Table 1)	-07 (ss)
	=133.6+07
Class No.	133.607

Voçational education in Financial economics	**332.071**
Financial economics	332
Vocational education (Table 1)	-071 (ss)
	=133+07
Class No.	332.071

Distance education in Economics	**330.071 5**
Economics	330
Distance education (Table 1)	-071 5 (ss)
	=330+071 5
Class No.	330.071 5

Research on Islam	**297.072**
Islam	297
Research (Table 1)	-072 (ss)
	=297+072
Class No.	297.072

Experimental research in Physics	**530.072 4**
Physics	530
Experimental research (Table 1)	-072 4 (ss)
	=530+072 4
Class No.	530.072 4

Statistical methods in Physical chemistry	**541.072 7**
Physical chemistry	541
Statistical methods (Table 1)	-072 7 (ss)
	=541+072 7
Class No.	541.072 7

Exhibition of Oil paintings	**751.450 74**
Oil Paintings	751.45
Exihibition (Table 1)	-074 (ss)
	=751.45+074
Class No.	751.450 74

Awards for Television media	**070.195 079**
Television media	070.195
Awards (Table 1)	-079 (ss)

	=070.195+079
Class No.	070.195 079

Athletics for Males	**796.081**
Athletics	796
Males (Table 1)	-081 (ss)
	=796+081
Class No.	796.081

Feminist Applied psychology	**158.082**
Applied psychology	158
Feminist (Women) (Table 1)	-082 (ss)
	=158+082
Class No.	158.082

Street music for Teenagers	**781.532 083 5**
Street music	781.532
Teenagers (Table 1)	-083 5 (ss)
	=781.532+083 5
Class No.	781.532 083 5

Sweaters in 13th century	**687.146 090 22**
Sweaters	687.146
13th century (Table 1)	-090 22 (ss)
	=687.146+090 22
Class No.	687.146 090 22

Library Classification systems in 1930's	**025.430 904 3**
Library Classification systems	025.43
1930's (Table 1)	-090 43 (ss)
	=025.43+090 43
Class No.	025.430 904 3

Islamic ethics in 16th century	**297.509 031**
Islamic ethics	297.5
16th century (Table 1)	-090 31 (ss)
	=297.5+090 31
Class No.	297.509 031

Use of standard subdivisions with two zeros

Generally standard subdivisions are to be used with one zero. If the 0 subdivisions of a number in a schedule are used for special purposes, use 001-009 for standard subdivisions. At a number of places in the schedule the 0 subdivisions have been used for other purposes. At such places instructions have also been provided to add standard subdivisions with two zeros. If the classifier has to add a standard subdivision to such a number where he/she is instructed to use double zero for ss, then he/she must use double zero. Some examples of using double zeros are illustrated in the next few pages.

Standards for Documentation	**025.002 18**
Documentation	025
Instruction	.001-.009
	Standard subdivisions
Standards (Table 1)	-021 8 (ss)
	=025+002 18
Class No.	025.002 18

Libraries in 13th century	**027.009 022**
Libraries	027
Instruction	.001-.009
	Standard subdivisions
13th century (Table 1)	-090 22 (ss)
	=027+009 022
Class No.	027.009 022

Research on Modern Eastern philosophy	**181.007 2**
Eastern philosophy	181
Instruction	.001-.008
	Standard subdivisions
Research (Table 1)	-072 (ss)
	=181+007 2
Class No.	181.007 2

Encyclopaedia of Christianity	**230.003**
Christianity	230
Instruction	.002-.003
	Standard subdivisions of Christianity
Encyclopaedia (Table 1)	-03 (ss)
	=230+003
Class No.	230.003

Models of Kinds of states	**321.002 28**
Kinds of states	321
Instruction	.001-.009
	Standard subdivisions
Models (Table 1)	-022 8 (ss)
	=321+002 28
Class No.	321.002 28

Classification of Political parties of U K	**324.241 001 2**
Political parties of U K	324.241
Instruction	.241 001-.241 009
	Standard subdivisions
Classification (Table 1)	-012 (ss)
	=324.241+001 2
Class No.	324.241 001 2

Scientific principles of Economic geography	**330.900 15**
Economic geography	330.9
Instruction	.900 1-.900 8
	Standard subdivisions
Scientific principles (Table 1)	-015 (ss)
	=330.9+001 5
Class No.	330.900 15

Journal of Personal finance	**332.024 005**
Personal finance	332.024
Instruction	.024 001-.024 007
	Standard subdivisions
Journal (Table 1)	-05 (ss)
	=332.024+005
Class No.	332.024 005

Descriptive research in Public Finance	**336.007 23**
Public Finance	336
Instruction	.007-.008
	Standard subdivisions
Descriptive research (Table 1)	-072 3 (ss)
	=336+007 23
Class No.	336.007 23

Correspondence courses in Private law	**346.007 15**
Private law	346
Instruction	.005-.008
	Standard subdivisions
	As modified under 342-347
Correspondence courses	-071 5 (ss)
	=346+071 5
Class No.	346.007 15

(Note the above instruction i.e. as modified under 342-347. And on reaching 342-347 it is found that ss 07 has not been modified. Hence you have to verify whether the ss has been modified or not before using the ss)

Use of maps in Military Science	**355.002 23**
Military Science	355
Instruction	.001-.009
	Standard subdivisions
Maps (Table 1)	-022 3 (ss)
	=355+002 23
Class No.	355.002 23

Computer applications to Insurance	**368.002 85**
Insurance	368
Instruction	.002-.005
	Standard subdivisions
Computer applications (Table 1)	-028 5 (ss)
	=368+002 85
Class No.	368.002 85

Concordance on Adult education	**374.003**
Adult education	374
Instruction	.003-.005
	Standard subdivisions
Concordance (Table 1)	-03 (ss)
	=374+003
Class No.	374.003

Standards for Water transportation	**387.002 18**
Water transportation	387
Instruction	.001-.009

	Standard subdivisions of water transportation
Standards (Table 1)	-021 8 (ss)
	=387+002 18
Class No.	387.002 18

Algebra in the middle ages	**512.009 02**
Algebra	512
Instruction	.001-.009
	Standard subdivisions
Middle ages (Table 1)	-090 2 (ss)
	=512+009 02
Class No.	512.009 02

Diagrams in Fluid mechanics	**532.002 23**
Fluid mechanics	532
Instruction	.001-.009
	Standard subdivisions
Diagrams (Table 1)	-022 3 (ss)
	=532+002 23
Class No.	532.002 3

Patents for Petrology	**552.002 72**
Petrology	552
Instruction	.001-.008
	Standard subdivisions
Patents (Table 1)	-027 2 (ss)
	=552+002 72
Class No.	552.002 72

Dictionary of Disease	**616.003**
Disease	616

Instruction	.003-.006
	Standard subdivisions
Dictionary (Table 1)	-03 (ss)
	=616+003
Class No.	616.003

Research on Surgery	**617.007 2**
Surgery	617
Instruction	.003-.007
	Standard subdivisions of Surgery
Research (Table I)	-072 (ss)
	=617+007 2
Class No.	617.007 2

Applied mechanics in 20th century	**620.100 904**
Applied mechanics	620.1
Instruction	.100 1-.100 9
	Standard subdivisions
20th century (Table 1)	-090 4 (ss)
	=620.1+009 04
Class No.	620.100 904

Teaching of Animal husbandry at University	**636.007 11**
Animal husbandry	636
Instruction	.001-.009
	Standard subdivisions
Teaching at University level (Table 1)	-071 1 (ss)
	=636+007 11
Class No.	636.007 11

Methodology for Textiles	**677.001**

Textiles	677
Instruction	.001-.009
	Standard subdivisions
Methodology (Table 1)	-01 (ss)
	=677+001
Class No.	677.001

Sacred music for grandparents	**781.700 853**
Sacred music	781.7
Instruction	.700 1-.700 9
	Standard subdivisions
Grandparents (Table 1)	-085 3 (ss)
	=781.7+008 53
Class No.	781.700 853

Encyclopaedia of Indian History	**954.003**
Adult education	954
Instruction	Add as instructed under 930-990
Encyclopaedia (Table 1)	-003
	=954+003
Class No.	954.003

(Note here as per instructions under 930-990, to the numbers of history schedule from 930-990 the standard subdivisions are to be used with double zeros)

Use of standard subdivisions with three zeros

If the 00 subdivisions of a number in the schedule are also used for special purposes, use 0001-0009 for standard subdivisions. Some examples have been provided below:

Standards for Subject headings	**025.490 002 18**
Subject headings	025.49

Instruction	.490 001-.490 009
	Standard subdivisions
Standards (Table 1)	-021 8 (ss)
	=025.49+000 218
Class No.	025.490 002 18

Computer Applications in Special libraries	**026.000 285**
Special libraries	026
Instruction	.000 1-.000 5
	Standard subdivisions
Computer Applications (Table 1)	-028 5 (ss)
	=026+000 285
Class No.	026.000 285

Study of Service tax	**336.278 000 71**
Service tax	336.278
Instruction	.278 000 1-.278 000 9
	Standard subdivisions
Study (Table 1)	-071 (ss)
	=336.278+000 71
Class No.	336.278 000 71

Models for Curricula	**375.000 228**
Curricula	375
Instruction	.000 1-.000 9
	Standard subdivisions
Models (Table 1)	-022 8 (ss)
	=375+000 228
Class No.	375.000 228

Management of Labour unions in Industries other than extractive, manufacturing, construction	**331.881 100 068**
Labour unions in Industries other than Extractive, manufacturing, construction	331.881 1
Instruction	.881 100 01-.881 100 09 Standard subdivisions
Management (Table 1)	-068 (ss) =331.881 1+000 68
Class No.	331.881 100 068

Encyclopaedia of Insurance law	**346.086 000 3**
Insurance law	346.086
Instruction	.086 000 1-.086 000 9 Standard subdivisions
Encyclopaedia (Table 1)	-03 (ss) =346.086+000 3
Class No.	346.086 000 3

Use of more than one standard subdivisions

In normal circumstances only one standard subdivision can be used. Do not add multiple standard subdivisions to the same number except when specifically instructed to do so, and in the following instances.

1. A standard subdivision may be added to standard subdivisions that have changed or extended meanings. For example, notation 03 from Table 1, the standard subdivision for encyclopaedias, may be added to 370.15 Educational psychology to represent encyclopaedias of educational psychology 370.1503 because the regular meaning of 370.15 (scientific principles) has been discontinued to 370.1 and replaced by an extended meaning of the standard subdivision for psychological principles at this number.

2. When standard subdivisions are displaced to nonzero numbers (usually for geographic treatment), the full range of standard subdivisions may be added. For example: the management of penal institutions in Great Britain 365.941068.

However there is a provision of adding second standard subdivision with 04 Special Topics (standard subdivision). This standard subdivision can be added only when it is specially set forth in the schedules. The second standard subdivision from 01 to 09 can be added to it and its subdivisions as required. Some examples are illustrated below:

Participatory democracy in India	**323.042 095 4**
Civil and political rights	323
Participatory democracy	.042 (ss)
2nd Standard subdivision	-09 (2nd ss)
India (Table 2)	-54
	=323+042+09+54
Class No.	323.042 095 4

Management of Job creation in labour market	**331.120 424 068**
Labour market	331.12
Job creation	.042 4 (ss)
Management (2nd Standard subdivision)	-068 (2nd ss)
	=331.12+042 4+068
Class No.	331.120 424 068

Encyclopaedia of Solid-state Chemistry	**541.042 103**
Physical chemistry	541
Solid state chemistry	.042 1 (ss)
Encyclopaedia (2nd Standard subdivision)	-03 (2nd ss)
	=541+042 1+03
Class No.	541.042 103

(Note .0421 (Solid-state Chemistry) is made as per the instructions at .042)

Research on Underground architecture	**720.473 072**
Architecture	720
Special topics	.4
Underground architecture	.473 (ss)
Research (2nd Standard subdivision)	-072 (2nd ss)
	=720+473+072
Class No.	720.473 072

Apart from above if any title requires application of more than one standard subdivision, then only one standard subdivision can be added. To decide which standard subdivision is to be added and which is to be avoided, the table of preference provided in volume 1 at the beginning of Table 1 (page no. 186) must be followed. The table of preference is provided below for reference.

Special topics	-04
Persons	-092
Auxiliary techniques and procedure; apparatus, equipment, materials	-028
Education, research, related topics (Except -074, -075)	-07
Management	-068
Philosophy and theory	-01
The subject as a profession, occupation, hobby	-023
The subject for persons in specific occupations	-024
Directories of persons and organizations	-025
Patents and identification marks	-027
Commercial miscellany	-029
Organizations	-0601-0609
Organizations (without subdivisions)	-06
History and description with respect to kinds of persons	-08

Treatment by specific continents, countries, localities; extraterrestrial worlds	-093-099
Treatment by areas, regions, places in general	-091
Maintenance and repair	-0288
Historical periods	-0901-0905
Forecasting and forecasts	-0112
Museums, collections, exhibits	-074
Museum activities and services Collecting	-075
Review and exercise	-076
Programmed texts	-077
Illustrations, models, miniatures	-022
Tabulated and related materials	021
Synopses and outlines	-0202
Humorous treatment	-0207
Audiovisual treatment	-0208
Language and communication	-014
Dictionaries, encyclopaedias, concordances	-03
Historical and geographical treatment (without subdivision)	-09
Serial publications	-05

Let us go through some examples:

Encyclopaedia of Research on Library science	**020.72**
Library science	020
Research (Table 1)	-072 (ss)
Encyclopaedia (Table 1)	-03 (ss)
	=020+072
Class No.	020.72

(Note here -07 has a preference over -03, as per table of preference and one zero of 020 has been removed as it is redundant)

Patents for Equipments in Chemical engineering	**660.028**
Chemical engineering	660
Equipments (Table 1)	-028 (ss)
Patents (Table 1)	-021 8 (ss)
	=660+028
Class No.	660.028
History of Teaching of Animal husbandry at University	**636.007 11**
Animal husbandry	636
Instruction	.001-.009
	Standard subdivisions
Teaching at University level (Table 1)	-071 1 (ss)
History (Table 1)	-09 (ss)
	=636+007 11
Class No.	636.007 11
Journal on Personnel management of Central Banks	**332.110 683**
Central Banks	332.11
Personnel management (Table 1)	-068 3 (ss)
Journal (Table 1)	-05 (ss)
	=332.11+068 3
Class No.	332.110 683
Study of Astrology in 19th Century	**133.607**
Astrology	133.6
Study (Table 1)	-071 (ss)
19th Century (Table 1)	-090 34 (ss)
	=133.6+071
Class No.	133.6071

Museum of 16th Century tales about horses	**398.245 296 655 090 31**
Base Number	398.245 2
Instruction	Add to base number 398.245 2 the numbers following 59 in 592-599; then add further as instructed under 398.21-398.27
Horses	~~59~~9.665 5
16th Century (Table 1)	-090 31(ss)
Museums (Table 1)	074(ss)
	=398.245 2+966 55+090 31
Class No.	398.245 296 655 090 31

Attention: You have been habitual of using Table 7 with standard subdivision 024 (The Subject for persons in specific occupations). The Table 7 has been removed from DDC 22. The numbers from the whole schedule i.e. 001 to 999 can be added to 024 in DDC 22. Hence the coverage is unlimited now instead of limited to a single table. Some examples are provided below.

Astrology for mathematicians	**133.602 451**
Astrology	133.6
The Subject for persons in specific occupations (Table 1)	-024 (ss)
Instruction	Add to base number -024 notation 001-999
Mathematics (Schedule)	510
	=133.6+024+51
Class No.	133.602 451

(Note here zero from 510 has been removed because this is only to make the class number of three digits long)

Algebra for Classifiers	**512.002 402 542**
Algebra	512
The Subject for persons in (Table 1) specific occupations	-024 (ss)
Instruction	Add to base number -024 notation 001-999
Classification (Schedule)	025.42
	=512+002 4+025.42
Class No.	512.002 402 542

Women psychology for Gynecologists	**155.633 024 618 1**
Women psychology	155.633
The Subject for persons in (Table 1) specific occupations	-024 (ss)
Instruction	Add to base number -024 notation 001-999
Gynecology (Schedule)	618.1
	=155.633+024+618.1
Class No.	155.633 024 618 1

Statistical mathematics for Cell biologists	**519.502 457 16**
Statistical mathematics	519.5
The Subject for persons in specific occupations (Table 1)	-024 (ss)
Instruction	Add to base number -024 notation 001-999
Cell biology (Schedule)	571.6
	= 519.5+024+571.6
Class No.	519.502 457 16

Grammar for English poets	**415.024 821**
Grammar	415
The Subject for persons in specific occupations (Table 1)	-024 (ss)
Instruction	Add to base number -024 notation 001-999
English poetry (Schedule)	821
	=415+024+821
Class No.	415.024 821

5
USE OF TABLE 2: AREAS

The Table 2 in DDC consists of notation for geographic areas, historical periods, persons. The numbers from Table 2 are never used alone, but may be used as required with any number from the schedules. These numbers can be added by three different ways viz. i. Direct use through instruction. ii. Through the standard subdivision -09, and iii. Through other tables. These ways are discussed with suitable examples in the next few pages.

ADDING AREAS WHEN THERE IS AN INSTRUCTION

At various places in the schedules, there are instruction regarding use of Table 2 i.e. Areas Table. In this case the area numbers are added directly from Table 2. For example in schedule of General libraries at the number 027.4 Public libraries there is such an instruction under 027.43-.49. The instruction reads as under.

Add to base number 027.4 notation 3-9 from Table 2.

This is an add note which instruct the classifier to add the numbers 3 to 9 from Table 2 to the base number 027.4. Here the classifier only have to act step by step according to instruction. For the convenience of the students these steps are illustrated below:

Suppose you have to classify a title "Public libraries in Haryana". You will find following add note at reaching the number 027.43-.49 in the schedule.

.4	Public libraries
.43-.49	Treatment by specific continents, countries. localities

Add to base number 027.4 notation 3-9 from Table 2.

You just follow the following steps and the class number is ready.

Step 1. Note down the base number. 027.4

Step 2. Go to Table 2 in volume 1 and search a number for Haryana between 3 to 9 -545 58

Step 3. Suffix the number taken from Table 2 to the base number 027.554558

(As a matter of mnemonic and convenience a blank space is provided after each three digits starting from the sixth digit. Hence our class number will look like: 027.554 558)

This is the first way of adding areas notation from Table 2. You have already made the class numbers using Table 2 from Law, and Geography and History schedules. Let us try more examples of the same nature.

National Library of India	**027.554**
National Libraries	027.5
Instruction	Add to base number 027.5 notation 3-9 from Table 2
India (Table 2)	-54
	=027.5+54
Class No.	027.554

School Libraries in Chhattisgarh	**027.854 137**
School Libraries	027.8
Instruction	Add to base number 027.8 notation 3-9 from Table 2
Chhattisgarh (Table 2)	-541 37
	=027.8+541 37
Class No.	027.854 137

College Libraries in Jharkhand	**027.754 127**
School Libraries	027.7
Instruction	Add to base number 027.7 notation 3-9 from Table 2
Jharkhand (Table 2)	-541 27
	=027.7+541 27
Class No.	027.754 127

The Times of India	**079.54**
Journalism and newspapers in other geographic areas	079
Instruction	Add to base number 079 notation 1-9 from Table 2
India (Table 2)	-54
	=079+54
Class No.	079.54

Language policy of New Zealand	**306.449 93**
Language planning and policy	306.449
Instruction	Add to base number 306.449 notation 4-9 from Table 2
New Zealand (Table 2)	-93
	=306.449+93
Class No.	306.449 93

Political conditions in Iraq	**320.956 7**
Political situation and conditions	320.9
Instruction	Add to base number 320.9 notation 01-9 from Table 2
Iraq (Table 2)	-567
	=320.9+567

Class No.	320.956 7

Political parties in Afghanistan	**324.258 1**
Political parties	324.2
Instruction	Add to base number 324.2 notation 4-9 from Table 2
Afghanistan (Table 2)	-581
	=324.2+581
Class No.	324.258 1

Communist party of India	**324.254 075**
Political parties	324.2
Instruction	Add to base number 324.2 notation 4-9 from Table 2; then add to the number according to the table below
India (Table 2)	-54
Communist parties	075
	=324.2+54+075
Class No.	324.254 075

Economic conditions of Pakistan	**330.954 91**
Economic situation and conditions	330.9
Instruction	Add to base number 330.9 notation 3-9 from Table 2
Pakistan (Table 2)	-5491
	=330.9+5491
Class No.	330.954 91

Crime and its alleviation in Assam	**364.954 162**
Historical, geographic, persons treatment of Crime and its alleviation	364.9

Instruction	Add to base number 364.9 notation 01-9 from Table 2
Assam (Table 2)	-541 62
	=364.9+541 62
Class No.	364.954 162

Higher education in Canada **378.71**

Higher education	378
Instruction	Add to base number 378 notation 4-9 from Table 2
Canada (Table 2)	-71
	=378+71
Class No.	378.71

Animals in South Africa **591.968**

Treatment of animals by specific continents, Countries, localities	591.9
Instruction	Add to base number 591.9 notation 3-9 from Table 2
South Africa (Table 2)	-68
	=591.9+68
Class No.	591.968

Management of restaurants in Spain **647.954 6**

Eating and drinking places	647.95
Instruction	Add to base number 647.95 notation 3-9 from Table 2
Spain (Table 2)	-46
	=647.95+46
Class No.	647.954 6

ADDING AREAS WHEN THERE IS NO INSTRUCTION

When there is no instruction regarding the use of area table in the schedule and there is a requirement of area number. In such a case the classifier can add the area number through the standard subdivision 09 Historical, geographic, persons treatment. There is a provision of adding areas table under standard subdivision 09. You will find instructions to this effect under -091, -092 2 and -093-099. The instructions read as under.

At -091	Add to base number -091 the numbers following -1 in notation 11-19 from Table 2
At -092 2	Add to base number -092 2 notation 3-9 from Table 2
At -093-099	Add to base number -09 notation 3-9 from Table 2; then add further as follows

Therefore, we can use areas table through the standard subdivision -09. In case you will use areas table through -091 & -093-099, you can add the numbers directly from Table 2 to the -09. But while adding areas number though -092 2, you have to add areas numbers to -092 2. The most important thing here to remember is that while adding areas through standard subdivision, you have to keep in mind the use of number of zeros. It depends on the instructions to this effect in the schedules. Let us try some examples.

Library networks in Developing countries	**021.650 917 24**
Library networks	021.65
Historical and geographic treatment (S.S.)	-09
Developing countries (Table 2)	-172 4
	=021.65+09+172 4
Class No.	021.650 917 24

Hinduism in Gujarat	**294.509 547 5**
Hinduism	294.5
Historical and geographic treatment (S.S.)	-09
Gujarat (Table 2)	-547 5
	=294.5+09+547 5
Class No.	294.509 547 5

Trade unions in Uttaranchal	**331.880 954 51**
Trade unions	331.88
Historical and geographic treatment (S.S.)	-09
Uttaranchal (Table 2)	-545 1
	=331.88+09+545 1
Class No.	331.880 954 51

Military training of officers in U K	**355.550 941**
Military training of officers	355.55
Historical and geographic treatment (S.S.)	-09
U K (Table 2)	-41
	=355.55+09+41
Class No.	355.550 941

Floods control in Finland	**363.349 360 948 97**
Floods control	363.349 36
Historical and geographic treatment (S.S.)	-09
Finland (Table 2)	-489 7
	=363.349 36+09+489 7
Class No.	363.349 360 948 97

Teacher-Parent relations in elementary schools in Kerala	**372.110 300 954 83**
Base Number	372.1
Instruction	Add to base number 372.1

the numbers following 371 in 371.1-371.8

Teacher-Parent relations ~~371~~.103

Historical & Geographic treatment (Table 1) -09

Kerala -548 3

=372.1+103+009+548 3

Class No. 372.110 300 954 83

(Pl. note here 00 is used for using ss, as it is provided under 371.1)

Variations in snow and snowfall over time in J&K **551.578 430 954 6**

Base Number 551.578 4

Instruction Add to base number 551.578 4 the numbers following 551.577 in 551.5771-551.5773

Variations over time ~~551.577~~ 3

Historical & Geographic treatment (Table 1) -09

J&K (Jammu and Kashmir) (Table 2) -546

=551.578 4+3+09+546

Class No. 551.578 430 954 6

Wheat crops in Bangladesh **633.110 954 92**

Wheat crops 633.11

Historical and geographic treatment (S.S.) -09

Bangladesh (Table 2) -549 2

=633.11+09+549 2

Class No. 633.110 954 92

Skim milk production in Saudi Arabia **637.147 095 38**

Skim milk production 637.147

Historical and geographic treatment (S.S.)	-09
Saudi Arabia (Table 2)	-538
	=637.147+09+538
Class No.	637.147 095 38

Manufacturing of rubber bands in Palestine	**678.350 956 94**
Manufacturing of rubber bands	678.35
Historical and geographic treatment (S.S.)	-09
Palestine (Table 2)	-569 4
	=678.35+09+569 4
Class No.	678.350 956 94

Interior Lighting in Prison Library building in Goa	**621.322 782 665 095 478**
Base Number	621.322
Instruction	Add to base number 621.322 the numbers following 72 in 725-728
Library building	~~72~~7.82
Instruction	Add to base number ~~72~~7.82 the numbers following 027 in 027.1-027.8
Prison Library	~~027~~.665
Historical and geographic treatment (S.S.)	-09 (ss)
Goa (Table 2)	-547 8
	=621.322+782+665+09+547 8
Class No.	621.322 782 665 095 478

Control of Scorpion flies in Tomatoes crops in Andhra Pradesh	**635.642 974 409 548 4**
Base Number (Tomatoes *)	635.642

Instruction — Except for modification shown under specific entries, add to each subdivision identified by * as follows:

Injuries, disease, pests — 9

Instruction — Add to 9 the numbers following 632 in 632.1-632.9

Insect pests — ~~632~~.7

Instruction — Add to base number ~~632~~.7 the numbers following 595.7 in 595.72-595.79

Scorpion flies — ~~595.7~~44

Historical and geographic treatment (S.S ` — -09 (ss)

Andhra Pradesh (Table 2) — -548 4

=635.642+9+7+44+09+548 4

Class No. — 635.642 974 409 548 4

Building for Mahabharata Museum in Delhi — **727.629 459 23**

Base Number — 727.6

Instruction — Add to base number 727.6 notation 001-999

Mahabharata — 294.592 3

Historical and geographic treatment (Table 1) — -09 (ss)

Delhi (Table 2) — -545 6

=727.6+294.592 3+09+545 6

Class No. — 727.629 459 230 954 56

Water transportation in Canada — **387.009 71**

Water transportation — 387

Instruction .001-.009

Standard subdivisions of water transportation

Historical and geographic treatment (S.S.) -09 (ss)

Canada (Table 2) -71

=387+009+71

Class No. 387.009 71

Treatment of Anemia by Radiotherapy in Japan **616.152 064 200 952**

Base Number (Anemia) 616.152

Instruction Except for modification shown under specific entries, add to each subdivision identified by * as follows:

Other therapies 062-069

Instruction Add to 06 the numbers following 615.8 in 615.82-615.89

Radiotherapy ~~615.8~~42

Historical & Geographic treatment (Table 1) -09

Japan (Table 2) -52

=616.152+06+42+009+52

Class No. 616.152 064 200 952

Plastic surgery of Face in Australia 617.520 592 009 4

Base Number (Face *) 617.52

Instruction Except for modification shown under specific entries, add to each subdivision identified by * as follows:

Plastic surgery	0592
Historical & Geographic treatment (Table 1)	-09
Australia (Table 2)	-94
	=617.52+059 2+009+94
Class No.	617.520 592 009 4

Diagnosis of Chickenpox among children in Maharashtra	**618.929 140 750 095 479**
Base Number	618.92
Instruction	Add to base number 618.92 the numbers following 616 in 616.1-616.9
Chickenpox *	~~616~~.914
Instruction	Except for modification shown under specific entries, add to each subdivision identified by * as follows:
Diagnosis	075
Historical & Geographic treatment (Table 1)	-09
Maharashtra (Table 2)	-547 9
	=618.92+914+075+009+547 9
Class No.	618.929 140 750 095 479

Treatment of Bacterial disease in Swines in Nagaland	**636.408 969 206 009 541 65**
Base Number	636.40
Instruction	Add to base number 636.40 the numbers following 636.0 in 636.001-636.08

Veterinary medicine	636.089
Instruction	Add to base number 636.089 the numbers following 61 in 610-618
Bacterial disease*	616.92
Instruction	Except for modification shown under specific entries, add to each subdivision identified by * as follows:
Treatment	06
Historical & Geographic treatment (Table 1)	-09
Nagaland (Table 2)	-541 65
	=636.40+89+692+06+009+541 65
Class No.	636.408 969 206 009 541 65

Special libraries in Australia	**026.000 994**
Special libraries	026
Instruction	.000 7-.000 9 Standard subdivisions
Historical and geographic treatment (S.S.)	-09 (ss)
Australia (Table 2)	-94
	=026+000 9+94
Class No.	026.000 994

Service tax in Brazil	**336.278 000 981**
Service tax	336.278
Instruction	.278 000 1-.278 000 9 Standard subdivisions
Historical and geographic treatment (S.S.)	-09 (ss)
Brazil (Table 2)	-81
	=336.278+000 9+81

Class No.	336.278 000 981

ADDING AREAS TABLE THROUGH OTHER TABLES

Areas table can also be added through other tables like Table 1 and Table 5. You have already seen the use of areas table through standard subdivision -09. This provision is general and classifier can add area notation through -09 on his own as and when required so. In Table 1, there are other instances where a provision of adding areas table is made. There is an instruction in the beginning of Table 5 also to add areas table to any number in Table 5. Let us try some examples.

Library and information science as a profession in India	**020.235 4**
Library and information science	020
Subject as a profession (Table 1)	-023
Instruction	Add to base number -023 notation 1-9 from Table 2
India (Table 2)	-54
	=020+23+54
Class No.	020.235 4

Patents on rice in USA	**633.180 272 73**
Rice	633.18
Patents (Table 1)	-027 2
Instruction	Add to base number -027 2 notation 1-9 from Table 2
USA (Table 2)	-73
	=633.18+0272+73
Class No.	633.180 272 73

Commercial miscellany of butter processing in UK	**637.202 941**

Butter processing	637.2
Commercial miscellany of Europe (Table 1)	-029 4
Instruction	Add to base number -029 4 the numbers following -4 in notation 41-49 from Table 2
UK (Table 2)	-41
	=637.2+029 4+1
Class No.	637.202 941

Research on Chemistry in Myanmar	**540.720591**
Chemistry	540
Research (Table 1)	-072
Instruction	Add to base number -072 0 notation 1-9 from Table 2
Myanmar (Table 2)	-591
	=540+72 0+591
Class No.	540.720 591

Competitions of Jumping in Korea	**796.432 079 519**
Jumping	796.432
Competitions (Table 1)	-079
Instruction	Add to base number -079 notation 4-9 from Table 2
Korea (Table 2)	-519
	=796.432+079+519
Class No.	796.432 079 519

Social status of Punjabis in UK	**305.891 420 41**
Social status of Ethnic and national groups	305.8
Instruction	Add to base number 305.8

	notation 05-9 from Table 5
Punjabis (Table 5)	-914 2
Instruction	Except where instructed otherwise, and unless it is redundant, add 0 to the number from this table and to the result add notation 1 or 3-9 from Table 2
U K (Table 2)	-41
	=305.8+914 2+0+41
Class No.	305.891 420 41

USE OF TWO NUMBERS FROM TABLE 2

There is a provision of adding two numbers from Table 2 to a number from schedules. One such option is provided under area table itself under -1 Areas, regions, places in general. Here the instruction reads as follows:

(Option: Add to each number in -1 as follows:

03-09 Treatment by continent, country, locality
Add to 0 notation 3-9 from Table 2

In this way we have an option to add two numbers from Table 2 to any number from the schedules. For example:

Rental libraries in rural areas of Haryana	**027.317 340 545 58**
Rental libraries	027.3
Instruction	Add to base number 027.3 notation 1-9 from Table 2
Rural areas (Table 2)	-173 4
Connecting digit	0
Haryana (Table 2)	-545 58
	=027.3+173 4+0+545 58
Class No.	027.317 340 545 58

Adult education in unaligned blocs of Gujarat	**374.917 160 547 5**
Adult education	374.9
Instruction	Add to base number 374.9 notation 01-9 from Table 2
Unaligned blocs (Table 2)	-171 6
Connecting digit	0
Gujarat (Table 2)	-547 5
	=374.9+171 6+0+547 5
Class No.	374.917 160 547 5

Maps of Forests of Himachal Pradesh	**912.191 520 545 2**
Maps	912.19
Instruction	Add to base number 912.19 the numbers following -1 in notation -11-19 from Table 2
Forests (Table 2)	-152
Connecting digit	0
Himachal Pradesh (Table 2)	-545 2
	=912.19+152+0+545 2
Class No.	912.191 520 545 2

In addition to this there are instructions at some places in the schedules to add two numbers from Table 2 and the connecting digit is 0. For example:

Foreign relations between China and U K	**327.510 41**
Foreign relations	327
Instruction	Add to base number 327 notation 01-9 from Table 2; then, for relations

	between that nation or region and another nation or region, add 0 and to the result add notation 1-9 from Table 2
China (Table 2)	-51
Connecting digit	0
U K (Table 2)	-41
	=327+51+0+41
Class No.	327.510 41

Foreign economic relations between Peru and USA **337.850 73**

Foreign economic relations	337
Instruction	Add to base number 337 notation 01-9 from Table 2; then, for relations between that nation or region and another nation or region, add 0 and to the result add notation 1-9 from Table 2
Peru (Table 2)	-85
Connecting digit	0
U S A (Table 2)	-73
	=337+85+0+73
Class No.	337.850 73

Cultural exchange between Sri Lanka and India **303.482 549 305 4**

Cultural exchange	303.482
Instruction	Add to base number 303.482 notation 1-9 from

	Table 2; then add 0 and then again add notation 1-9 from Table 2
Sri Lanka (Table 2)	-5493
Connecting digit	0
India (Table 2)	-54
	=303.482+5493+0+54
Class No.	303.482 549 305 4

Migration from Punjab to Canada 304.854 552 071

Migration	304.8
Instruction	Add to base number 304.8 notation 3-9 from Table 2; then add 0 and to the result add notation 1-9 from Table 2
Punjab (Table 2)	-545 52
Connecting digit	0
Canada (Table 2)	-71
	=304.8+545 52+0+71
Class No.	304.854 552 071

British educational aid to Pakistan 379.129 549 104 1

Educational aid	379.129
Instruction	Add to base number 379.129 notation 1-9 from Table 2; then for area providing support, add 0 and again add notation 1-9 from Table 2
Pakistan (Table 2)	-549 1
Connecting digit	0
British (Table 2)	-41
	=379.129+549 1+0+41
Class No.	379.129 549 104 1

USE OF TABLE 3
SUBDIVISIONS FOR THE ARTS FOR INDIVIDUAI LITERATURES, FOR SPECIFIC LITERARY FORMS

The Table 3 in DDC consists of notations for the arts, fo individual literatures, and for specific literary forms. Like othe tables in DDC this table is also never used alone, but may b used as required by add notes under subdivisions of individua literatures or with base numbers for individual literature identified by * under 810-890. It is clearly mentioned in th beginning of the table that the notation from this table can be used only with subdivisions of individual literature, which are identified with *. Hence you have to make it sure that the subdivision of individual literature to which you are adding notation from Table 3 must have been identified with. The subdivisions of individual literature which are not identified with * ends with language notation. Notation from Table 3 may also be used where instructed in 700.4, 791.4, 808-809.

The Table 3 is further divided into three subtables viz.:

1. Table 3A for description, critical appraisal, biography, single or collected works of an individual author.
2. Table 3B for description, critical appraisal, biography, single or collected works of two or more authors; also for rhetoric in specific literary forms.
3. Table 3C for additional elements used in number building

within Table 3B and as instructed in 704, 791.4, 808,809.

The class numbers of literature is made from different elements viz. Base number; form; period; kind; scope, or medium; notation 08 collections or notation 09 criticism; subform; additional notation from Table 3C and other tables. Any literary work could be of one of two types i.e. either it is written by single author or by more than one author. Both these categories have their different procedures for number building. Let us understand these procedures in the form of flow chart at next page.

The procedure explained in the flow chart form is described at the beginning of Table 3A and 3B. This procedure is explained there as step-by-step procedure. In this procedure the classifier has to take a decision at every crossing. The procedure provided under Table 3A is as under:

1. Look in the schedule 810-890 to find the base number for the language. The base number may be identified in an add note, e.g. at 820.1-828 ("add to base number 82") or another note, e.g., at 896 ("896.392 Swahili"); otherwise, it is the number given for the literature, e.g. Dutch-language literature 839.31. If there is a specific literary form, go to step 2; if not, go to the instructions under -8 in Table 3A.
2. In Table 3A find the correct subdivision for the literary form, e.g. poetry-1. Add this to base number, e.g. Swahili poetry 896.392 1, Dutch poetry 839.311. If the literary form appears as a subdivision of -8 Miscellaneous writings, go to the instructions under-8 in Table 3A; otherwise go to step 3.
3. Turn back to the appropriate number in the schedule 810-890 to see whether there is an applicable period table. If there is one, go to step 4; if not, complete the class number by inserting a point between third and fourth digits, e.g. Khmer (Cambodian) poetry by a 20th Century author 895.9321.

FLOW CHART FOR WORKS BY OR ABOUT AN INDIVIDUAL AUTHOR

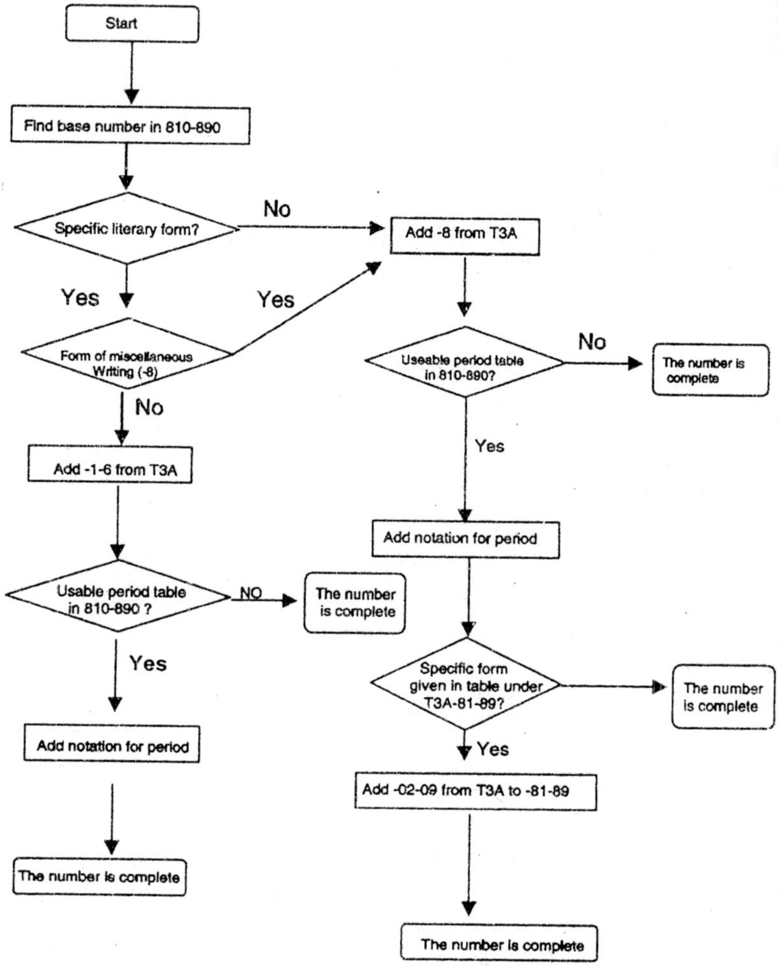

FLOW CHART FOR WORKS BY OR ABOUT MORE THAN ONE AUTHOR

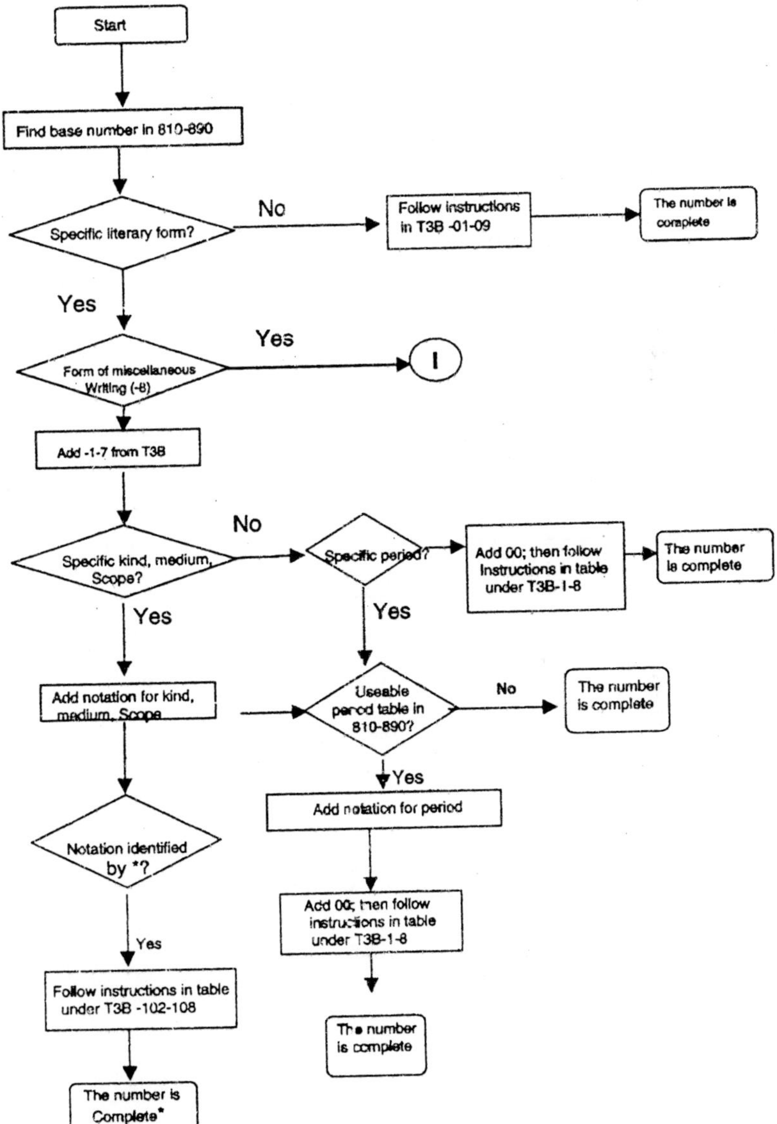

* If appropriate, standard subdivisions may be added

FLOW CHART FOR NOTATION 8 MISCELLANEOUS WRITINGS

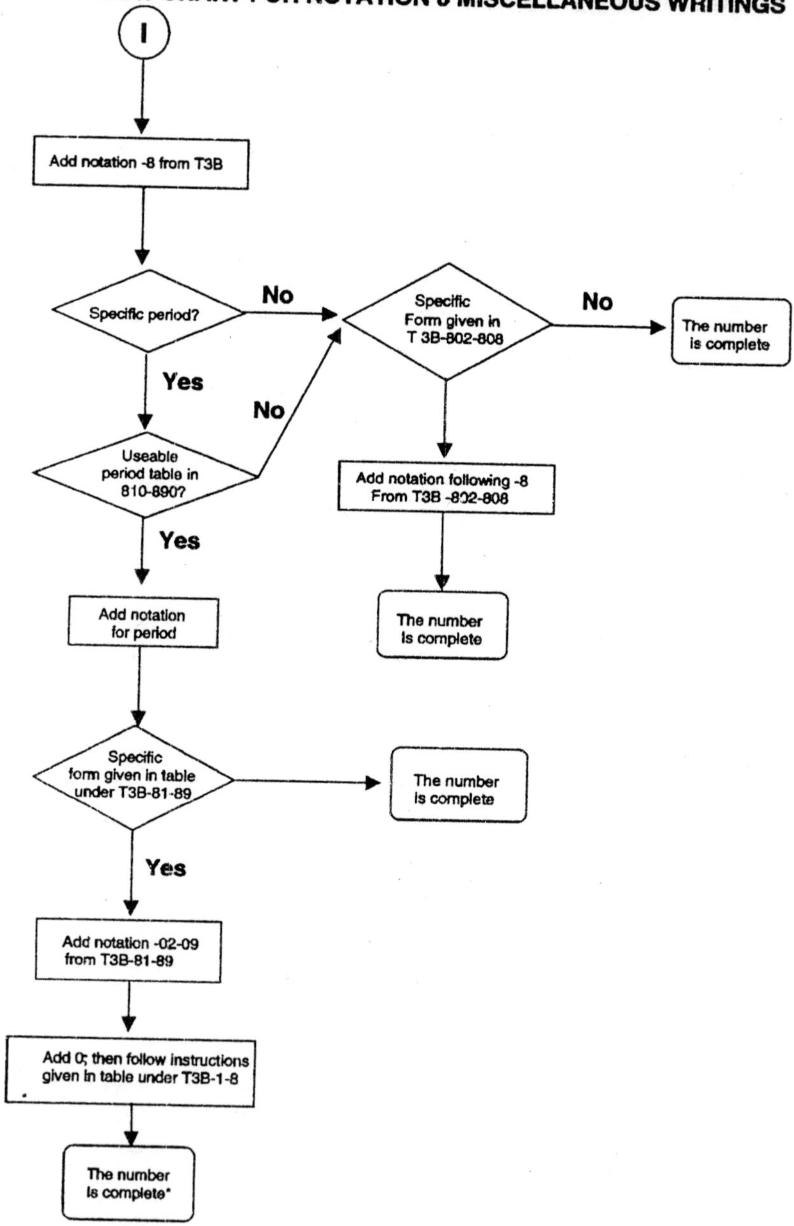

* If appropriate, standard subdivisions may be added

4. Select the appropriate period number. Add this number to the number already derived; always insert a point after the third digit. The class number is complete (except for William Shakespeare), since standard subdivisions are never added for individual authors, e.g. Spenser's Faerie Queene 821.3 (821 English Poetry + 3 Elizabethan period).

The procedure provided under Table 3B is as under:

1. Look in the schedule 810-890 to find the base number for the language. The base number may be identified in an add note, e.g. at 820.1-828 ("add to base number 82") or another note, e.g., at 896 ("896.392 Swahili"); otherwise, it is the number given for the literature, e.g. Dutch-language literature 839.31. If there is a specific literary form, go to step 2; if not, go to step 8.
2. In Table 3B find the subdivision for the literary form, e.g. English poetry 821, Dutch poetry 839.311. If the literary form appears as a subdivision of -8 Miscellaneous writings, go to the instructions under -8 in Table 3B. If the work deals with poetry, drama, fiction, or speech of specific media, scopes, kinds for which there is special notation in Table 3B (e.g., -1042 sonnets), go to step 3. For other works that deals with or fall within a limited time span, go to step 4. A limited time span is (1) fewer than three literary periods or (2) a single century. For other works not limited by time period, go to step 7.
3. Use the notation in Table 3B for the kind of poetry, drama, fiction, or speech, e.g. sonnets in English literature 821.042. Insert a point after the third digit. Check whether the specific form is (1) the sole kind in a heading identified by * or (2) is named in a subdivisions-are-added note as a kind for which subdivisions may be added or (3) appears in a class-here note under a heading identified by *. If note of these conditions holds, the number is complete, e.g. collections of English-language clerihews 821.07. If

one of the three conditions does not hold, follow the instructions in the table under -102-107 in Table 3B. Following these instructions will involve using Table 3C for literature of specific periods, literature displaying specific features or emphasizing specific subjects, and literature for and by specific kinds of persons, e.g., collections of English sonnets 821.042 08, collections of English sonnets about love 821.042 083 543.

4. Turn back to the appropriate number in the schedule 810-890 to see whether there is an applicable period table. If there is one, go to step 5; if not, complete the class number by inserting a point between third and fourth digit, e.g. Khmer (Cambodian) poetry by 20th Century authors 895.9321.

5. Select the appropriate period number. Add this number to the number already derived, e.g. English poetry of Elizabethan period 821.3; always insert a point after the third digit. Go to step 6.

6. Under the number for the literary form in Table 3B, go to the subdivisions for specific periods, e.g., under -1 for poetry go to -11-19. Follow the instructions given there, which will lead to use of the table under -1-8. For literature displaying specific features, literature emphasizing subjects, and literature for and by specific kinds of persons, the instructions at-1-8 will lead to use of Table 3C, e.g., critical appraisal of idealism in English Elizabethan poetry 821 30913.

7. If the work is not limited by time period, go to the first subdivisions under the particular form in Table 3B, e.g., under -1 for poetry go to 1001-1009. Follow the instructions given there, which will lead to the use of table under -1-8. For literature displaying specific features, literature emphasizing subjects, and literature for and by specific kinds of persons, the instructions at -1-8 will lead

to use of Table 3C, e.g., collections of English poetry by rural authors 821.008091734.

8. If the work is not limited to a specific literary form, consult -01-09 in Table 3B. Follow the instructions at the number selected, making use of Table 3C when specified, e.g., collections of English literature in many forms about holidays 820.80334. Use period notation 08001-08009 and -09001-09009 only if there is an applicable period table.

The procedure is well explained with examples and it can be easily followed. The examples of use of Table 3A, 3B, & 3C are provided in the following pages.

English poetry by a Nineteenth century author	**821.8**
Base number	82
Poetry (Table 3A)	-1
Nineteenth century (Table under 820.1-828)	8
	=82+1+8
Class No.	821.8

German drama by a fourteenth century author	**832.22**
Base number	83
Drama (Table 3A)	-2
Fourteenth century (Table under 830.1-838)	22
	=83+2+22
Class No.	832.22

French fiction by a classical period author	**843.4**
Base number	84
Fiction (Table 3A)	-3
Classical period (Table under 840.1-848)	4
	=84+3+4
Class No.	843.4

Catalan essays by a golden period author **849.943**

Base number 849.9

Essays (Table 3A) -4

Golden period (Table under 849.9) 3

=849.9+4+3

Class No. 849.943

Italian speeches by a romantic period author **855.7**

Base number 85

Speeches (Table 3A) -5

Romantic period (Table under 850.1-858) 7

=85+5+7

Class No. 855.7

Collections of Punjabi Sonnets about love **891.421 042 083 543**

Base number 891.42

Sonnets (Table 3B) -104 2

Collections (Table 3B) -08

Instruction Add to 08 notation 001-99 from Table 3C

Love (Table 3C) -354 3

=891.42+104 2+08+354 3

Class No. 891.421 042 083 543

Collections of Hindi Poetry on Holidays **891.431 008 033 4**

Base number 891.43

Poetry (Table 3B) -1

Instruction Add to -100 as instructed under -1-8.

Collections displaying specific features 801-809

Instruction Add to 80 notation 1-9 from Table 3C

Holidays (Table 3C)	-334
	=891.43+100+80+334
Class No.	891.431 008 033 4

Goa as depicted in Bengali Poetry	**891.441 008 032 547 8**
Base number	891.44
Poetry (Table 3B)	-1
Instruction	Add to -100 as instructed under -1-8.
Collections displaying specific features	801-809
Instruction	Add to 80 notation 1-9 from Table 3C
Places (Table 3C)	-32
Instruction	Add to -32 notation 1-9 from Table 2
Goa (Table 2)	-547 8
	=891.44+100+80+32+547 8
Class No.	891.441 008 032 547 8

Collections of French drama on pets	**842.008 036 2**
Base number	84
Drama (Table 3B)	-2
Instruction	Add to -200 as instructed under -1-8.
Collections displaying specific features	801-809
Instruction	Add to 80 notation 1-9 from Table 3C
Pets (Table 3C)	-362
	=84+200+80+362
Class No.	842.008 036 2

Collected Biography of Italian poets **851.009**

Base number	85
Poetry (Table 3B)	-1
Instruction	Add to -100 as instructed under -1-8.
History, description, critical appraisal Class here collected biography	-9
	=85+100+9
Class No.	851.009

Collections of Russian novels by rural authors **891.730 080 917 34**

Base number	891.7
Novels (Table 3B)	-3
Instruction	Add to -300 as instructed under -1-8.
Collections displaying specific features	801-809
Instruction	Add to 80 notation 1-9 from Table 3C
Literature for and by persons resident (Table 3C) in specific regions	- 91
Instruction	Add to -91 the numbers following -1 in notation -11-19 from Table 2
Rural (Table 2)	-173 4
	=891.7+300+80+91+173 4
Class No.	891.730 080 917 34

Collections of Oriya literature displaying God **891.456 080 382 021 1**

Base number	891.456
Collections of literary text (Table 3B)	-08
Instruction	Add to -080 notation 001-99 from Table 3C

Religious themes (Table 3C)	-382
Instruction	Add to base number -382 the numbers following 2 in 201-290
God	202.11
	=891.456+080+382+021 1
Class No.	891.456 080 382 021 1

Collections of Urdu literature produced by Assamese	**891.439 080 891 45**
Base number	891.439
Collections of literary text (Table 3B)	-08
Instruction	Add to -080 notation 001-99 from Table 3C
Literature for and by persons of (Table 3C) ethnic and national groups	- 8
Instruction	Add to -8 notation 05-99 from Table 5
Assamese (Table 5)	-914 5
	=891.439+080+8+914 5
Class No.	891.439 080 891 45

The collections of literary texts from more than two literatures are to be classified under 808. A few examples are as under:-

Collections of lyric poetry	**808.814**
Base number	808.81
Instruction	Add to base number 808.81 the numbers following -10 in notation 102-107 from Table 3B
Lyric poetry (Table 3B)	-104
	=808.81+4

Class No. 808.814

Collections of poetry on sex **808.819 353 8**

Base number 808.819

Instruction Add to base number 808.819 notation 1-3 from Table 3C

Sex (Table 3C) -353 8

=808.819+353 8

Class No. 808.819 353 8

Collections of One act plays **808.824 1**

Base number 808.82

Instruction Add to base number 808.82 the numbers following -20 in 202-205 from Table 3B

On act play (Table 3B) -~~20~~4 1

=808.82+41

Class No. 808.824 1

Collections of fiction displaying birth **808.839 354**

Base number 808.839

Instruction Add to base number 808.839 notation 1-3 from Table 3C

Birth (Table 3C) -354

=808.839+354

Class No. 808.839 354

Collections of narrative essays **808.849 23**

Base number 808.849

Instruction Add to base number

	808.849 notation 1-3 from Table 3C
Narrative (Table 3C)	-23
	=808.849+23
Class No.	808.849 23
Collections of public speeches	**808.851**
Base number	808.85
Instruction	Add to base number 808.85 the numbers following -50 in 501-506 from Table 3B
Public speeches (Table 3B)	-~~50~~1
	=808.85+1
Class No.	808.851
Collections of letters displaying friendship	**808.869 353**
Base number	808.869
Instruction	Add to base number 808.869 notation 1-3 from Table 3C
Friendship (Table 3C)	-353
	=808.869+353
Class No.	808.869 353
Collections of literary humor about customs	**808.879 355 9**
Base number	808.879
Instruction	Add to base number 808.879 notation 1-3 from Table 3C
Customs (Table 3C)	-355 9
	=808.879+355 9
Class No.	808.879 355 9

7

USE OF TABLE 4: SUBDIVISIONS OF INDIVIDUAL LANGUAGES AND LANGUAGE FAMILIES

In DDC the Table 4 consists of notations for subdivisions of individual languages and language families. Like other tables in DDC this table is also never used alone, but may be used as required by add notes under subdivisions of specific languages and language families, or with the base numbers for individual languages identified with * as explained under 420-490. Notation from Table 1 can be added to the notation in Table 4 when appropriate. The classifier should be sure before using Table 4 that the notation for the language either should be identified with * or there must be some add note regard to use of Table 4. Examples of use of Table 4 are provided in next few pages.

A book on English Acronyms	**421.1**
Base number	42
Acronyms (Table 4)	-11
	=42+11
Class No.	421.1

Use of nouns in German language	**435.54**
Base number	43

Nouns (Table 4)	-554
	=43+554
Class No.	435.54

Bengali words	**491.448 1**
Base number	491.44
Words (Table 4)	-81
	=491.44+81
Class No.	491.448 1

Spellings and pronunciation in Danish language	**439.818 13**
Base number	439.81
Spellings and pronunciation (Table 4)	-813
	=439.81+813
Class No.	439.818 13

Russian Primers	**491.786**
Base number	491.7
Primers {Readers} (Table 4)	-86
	=491.7+86
Class No.	491.786

Etymology of Hebrew language	**492.42**
Base number	492.4
Etymology (Table 4)	-2
	=492.4+2
Class No.	492.42

Swedish phonology	**439.715**
Base number	439.7
Phonology (Table 4)	-15

	=439.7+15
Class No.	439.715

English Dictionary	**423**
Base number	42
Dictionary (Table 4)	-3
	=42+3
Class No.	423

Dictionary of Bihari idioms	**491.454 313**
Base number	491.454
Dictionary of idioms (Table 4)	-313
	=491.454+313
Class No.	491.454 313

Picture Dictionary of Old Persian language	**491.513 17**
Base number	491.51
Picture Dictionary (Table 4)	-317
	=491.51+317
Class No.	491.513 17

Dictionary of abbreviations in Japanese	**495.631 5**
Base number	495.6
Dictionary of abbreviations (Table 4)	-315
	=495.6+315
Class No.	495.631 5

Dictionary of homonyms in Korean language	**495.731**
Base number	495.7
Dictionary of homonyms (Table 4)	-31
	=495.7+31
Class No.	495.731

Meaning of words in Burmese language	**495.881**
Base number	495.881
Meaning of words (Table 4)	-81
	=495.8+81
Class No.	495.881

Foreign element in French language	**442.4**
Base number	44
Foreign elements (Table 4)	-24
	=44+24
Class No.	442. 4

Sanskrit words in English language	**422.491 2**
Base number	42
Foreign elements (Table 4)	-24
Instruction	Add to -24 notation 1-9 from Table 6
Sanskrit language (Table 6)	-912
	=42+24+912
Class No.	422.491 2

Hindi words in Marathi language	**491.462 491 431**
Base number	491.46
Foreign elements (Table 4)	-24
Instruction	Add to -24 notation 1-9 from Table 6
Hindi language (Table 6)	-914 31
	=491.46+24+914 31
Class No.	491.462 491 431

Alphabets in Rajasthani language	**491.479 11**
Base number	491.479

Alphabets (Table 4)	-11
	=491.479+11
Class No.	491.479 11

Use of English words in French language **442.421**

Base number	44
Foreign elements (Table 4)	-24
Instruction	Add to -24 notation 1-9 from Table 6
English language (Table 6)	-21
	=44+24+21
Class No.	442.421

Translating from Sanskrit into Panjabi language **491.428 029 12**

Base number	491.42
Translating to and from other language (Table 4)	-802
Instruction	Add to -802 notation 2-9 from Table 6 for the language being translated from
Sanskrit language (Table 6)	-912
	=491.42+802+912
Class No.	491.428 029 12

Translating from Latin into Hindi language **491.438 027 1**

Base number	491.43
Translating to and from other language (Table 4)	-802
Instruction	Add to -802 notation 2-9 from Table 6 for the

	language being translated from
Latin language (Table 6)	-71
	=491.43+802+71
Class No.	491.438 027 1

Structural approach to expression of Hindi for Sindhi speaking people **491.438 249 141 1**

Base number	491.43
Structural approach to expression for (Table 4) Persons whose native language is different	-824
Instruction	Add to -824 notation 2-9 from Table 6
Sindhi language (Table 6)	-914 11
	=491.43+824+914 11
Class No.	491.438 249 141 1

Structural approach to expression of German for Tamil speaking people **438.249 481 1**

Base number	43
Structural approach to expression for (Table 4) Persons whose native language is different	-824
Instruction	Add to -824 notation 2-9 from Table 6
Tamil language (Table 6)	-948 11
	=43+824+948 11
Class No.	438.249 481 1

Audio-lingual approach to expression of Italian for Telugu speaking people **458.349 482 7**

Base number	45

Audio-lingual approach to expression for (Table 4) Persons whose native language is different	-834
Instruction	Add to -834 notation 2-9 from Table 6
Telugu language (Table 6)	-948 27
	=45+834+948 27
Class No.	458.349 482 7

Audio-lingual approach to expression of Spanish for Tibetan speaking people	**468.349 541**
Base number	46
Audio-lingual approach to expression for (Table 4) Persons whose native language is different	-834
Instruction	Add to -834 notation 2-9 from Table 6
Tibetan language (Table 6)	-954 1
	=46+834+954 1
Class No.	468.349 541

English-language DDC classification Reader for persons whose native language is not English	**428.640 240 254 31**
Base number	42
Readers for persons in specific occupations (Table 4)	-864 024
Instruction	Add to -864024 notation 001-999
DDC classification (from schedule)	025.431
	=42+864 024+025 431
Class No.	428.640 240 254 31

Hindi-language Artificial intelligence Reader for persons whose native language is not Hindi **491.438 640 240 063**

Base number	491.43
Readers for persons in (Table 4) specific occupations	-864 024
Instruction	Add to -864024 notation 001-999
Artificial intelligence (from schedule)	006.3
	=491.43+864 024+006.3
Class No.	491.438 640 240 063

French-language primer for peoples whose native language is Hindi **438.649 143 1**

Base number	43
Readers for specific native (Table 4) language speakers	-864
Instruction	Add to -864 notation 2-9 from Table 6
Hindi language (Table 6)	-914 31
	=43+864+914 31
Class No.	438.649 143 1

Telugu-language primer for peoples whose native language is Tamil **494.827 864 948 11**

Base number	494.827
Readers for specific native (Table 4) language speakers	-864
Instruction	Add to -864 notation 2-9 from Table 6

Tamil language (Table 6)	-948 11
	=494.827+864+948 11
Class No.	494.827 864 948 11

Telugu-language primer of cricket for peoples whose native language is Tamil **494.827 864 948 110 24 796 358**

Base number	494.827
Readers for specific native language speakers (Table 4)	-864
Instruction	Add to -864 notation 2-9 from Table 6; then add further as follows
Tamil language (Table 6)	-948 11
Readers for persons in specific occupations	024
Instruction	Add to base number 024 notation 001-999
Cricket (from Schedule)	796.358
	=494.827+864+948 11+024+796.358
Class No.	494.827 864 948 110 247 963 58

Russian-language primer on Income Tax for peoples whose native language is Hindi **491.7864 914 310 243 430 52**

Base number	491.7
Readers for specific native language speakers (Table 4)	-864
Instruction	Add to -864 notation 2-9 from Table 6; then add further as follows
Hindi language (Table 6)	-914 31

Readers for persons in specific occupations 024

Instruction Add to base number 024 notation 001-999

Income Tax (from Schedule) 343.052

=491.7+864+914 31+024+343.052

Class No. 491.786 914 310 243 430 52

Indian systems of signing and fingerspelling of English **428.915 4**

Base number 42

Specific systems of manual coding (Table 4) -891

Instruction Add to -891 notation 4-9 from Table 2

India (Table 2) -54

=42+891+54

Class No. 428.915 4

Bilingual dictionaries: A bilingual dictionary is one that gives words in one language and its meaning in a different language. As there are two languages involved, hence notation for both language should be used. Now the question arises which language should come first and which later. There is a specific provision for this problem in DDC. The provision is as under:-

1. A bilingual dictionary with entry words in only one language is classed with that language.
2. A bilingual dictionary with entry words in both languages is classed with the language in which it will be more useful. According to this provision "less known" or "less popular" language should come first.
3. If both the languages are equally less or more popular, then give priority to the language coming later in 420-490.

Let us try some examples.

English-French Dictionary 423.41

Base number	42
Dictionary (Table 4)	-3
Instruction	Add to -3 notation 2-9 from Table 6
French Language (Table 6)	-41
	=42+3+41
Class No.	423.41

(Note: Entry words are in only one language)

Rajpal Learners' Hindi-English Dictionary **423.914 31**

Base number	42
Dictionary (Table 4)	-3
Instruction	Add to -3 notation 2-9 from Table 6
Hindi Language (Table 6)	-914 31
	=42+3+914 31
Class No.	423.914 31

(Note: English is less popular language in India)

Sanskrit- Hindi Dictionary **491.239 143 1**

Base number	491.2
Dictionary (Table 4)	-3
Instruction	Add to -3 notation 2-9 from Table 6
Hindi Language (Table 6)	-914 31
	=491.2+3+914 31
Class No.	491.239 143 1

(Note: Sanskrit is less popular language in India)

German- French Dictionary **443.31**

Base number	44

Dictionary (Table 4)	-3
Instruction	Add to -3 notation 2-9 from Table 6
German Language (Table 6)	-31
	=44+3+31
Class No.	443.31

(Note: Both languages are more or less equally popular languages in India, hence the language coming later in the schedule is taken first).

8

USE OF TABLE 5: ETHNIC AND NATIONAL GROUPS

In DDC the Table 5 consists of notations for ethnic and national groups. Like other tables in DDC this table is also never used alone, but may be used as required by add notes or through the interposition of notation 089 from Table 1. There are certain provisions, which require an attention. These are as under:-

1. Except where instructed otherwise, and unless it is redundant, add 0 to the number from this table and to the result add notation 1 or 3-9 from Table 2 for area in which a group is or was located.
2. Standard subdivisions may be added to Table 5 notation when that notation is added directly to the base number. In other words standard subdivisions may be added to the notation from Table 5 when it is added through add note and not through interposition of 089 from Table 1.
3. When notation from Table 5 is not followed by 0 plus notation from Table 2, use 00 for standard subdivision. This is to avoid the confusion whether it is a Table 5 notation or a standard subdivision.
4. Except where instructed otherwise, give preference to the ethnic group over nationality.
5. Except where instructed otherwise, when choosing between two ethnic groups, give preference to the group for which the notation is different from that for the nationality of the people.
6. Except where instructed otherwise, when choosing between

two national groups, give preference to the former or ancestral national group.

Examples of use of Table 5 are provided in next few pages.

Ethno psychology of Mongols	**155.849 42**
Base number	155.84
Instruction	Add to base number 155.84 notation 05-9 from Table 5
Mongols (Table 5)	-942
	=155.84+942
Class No.	155.849 42

Public opinions of Italians	**303.387 51**
Base number	303.387
Instruction	Add to base number 303.387 notation 1-9 from Table 5
Italians (Table 5)	-51
	=303.387+51
Class No.	303.387 51

Social status of Panjabis	**305.891 42**
Base number	305.8
Instruction (at .805-.89)	Add to base number 305.8 notation 05-9 from Table 5
Panjabis (Table 5)	-914 2
	=305.8+914 2
Class No.	305.891 42

Civil rights of Arabs	**323.119 27**
Base number	323.11

Instruction	Add to base number 323.11 notation 1-9 from Table 5
Arabs (Table 5)	-927
	=323.11+927
Class No.	323.119 27

Ethnic cookery of Kurds	**641.592 915 97**
Base number	641.592
Instruction	Add to base number 641.592 notation 05-9 from Table 5
Kurds (Table 5)	-915 97
	=641.592+915 97
Class No.	641.592 915 97

Art of Thai people	**704.039 591 1**
Base number	704.03
Instruction	Add to base number 704.03 notation 05-9 from Table 5
Thai (Table 5)	-959 11
	=704.03+959 11
Class No.	704.039 591 1

World history of Persians	**909.049 155**
Base number	909.04
Instruction	Add to base number 909.04 notation 05-9 from Table 5
Persians (Table 5)	-915 5
	=909.04+915 5
Class No.	909.049 155

Ethno psychology of Italians in China	**155.845 105 1**
Base number	155.84
Instruction	Add to base number 155.84 notation 05-9 from Table 5
Italians (Table 5)	-51
Connecting digit	0
China (Table 2)	-51
	=155.84+51+0+51
Class No.	155.845 105 1

Public opinions of Mongols in Iraq	**303.387 942 056 7**
Base number	303.387
Instruction	Add to base number 303.387 notation 1-9 from Table 5
Mongols (Table 5)	- 942
Connecting digit	0
Iraq (Table 2)	- 567
	=303.387+942+0+567
Class No.	303.387 942 056 7

Social status of Panjabis in Canada	**305.891 420 71**
Base number	305.8
Instruction (at .805-.89)	Add to base number 305.8 notation 05-9 from Table 5
Panjabis (Tabie 5)	-914 2
Connecting digit	0
Canada (Table 2)	-71
	=305.8+914 2+0+71
Class No.	305.891 420 71

Civil rights of Indians in Pakistan	**323.119 141 105 491**
Base number*	323.11
Instruction	Add to base number 323.11 notation 1-9 from Table 5
Indians (Table 5)	-914 11
Connecting digit	0
Pakistan (Table 2)	-549 1
	=323.11+914 11+0+549 1
Class No.	323.119 141 105 491

Libraries in the regions where Sinhalese predominate	**027.017 491 48**
Base number	027.0
Instruction (at .01-.09)	Add to base number 027.0 the notation 1-9 from Table 2
Regions where specific ethnic and national groups predominate (Table 2)	-174
Instruction	Add to base number -174 notation 05-9 from Table 5
Sinhalese (Table 5)	-914 8
	=027.0+174+914 8
Class No.	027.017 491 48

Economic history of regions where Gypsies predominate	**330.917 491 497**
Base number	330.91
Instruction	Add to base number 330.91 the number following -1 in notation

11-19 from Table 2

Regions where specific ethnic (Table 2) and national groups predominate -174

Instruction Add to base number -174 notation 05-9 from Table 5

Gypsies {Romany people} (Table 5) -914 97

=330.91+74+914 97

Class No. 330.917 491 497

Ethnic cookery of Irish in Iran **641.592 916 205 5**

Base number 641.592

Instruction Add to base number 641.592 notation 05-9 from Table 5

Irish (Table 5) -916 2

Connecting digit 0

Iran (Table 2) -55

=641.592+916 2+0+55

Class No. 641.592 916 205 5

Art of Bengalis in India **704.039 144 054**

Base number 704.03

Instruction Add to base number 704.03 notation 05-9 from Table 5

Bengalis (Table 5) -914 4

Connecting digit 0

India (Table 2) -54

=704.03+914 4+0+54

Class No. 704.039 144 054

Bulgarians folk music	**781.629 181 1**
Base number	781.62
Instruction	Add to base number 781.62 notation 05-99 from Table 5
Bulgarians (Table 5)	-918 11
	=781.62+918 11
Class No.	781.629 181 1

Collections of literature by Burmese	**808.898 958**
Base number	808.89
Instruction	Add to base number 808.89 notation -8-9 from Table 3C
Literature for and by persons of ethnic and national groups (Table 3C)	-8
Instruction	Add to -8 notation 05-99 from Table 5
Burmese (Table 5)	-958
	=808.89+8+958
Class No.	808.898 958

Biographies of Marathas	**920.009 294 8**
Base number	920.009 2
Instruction	Add to base number 920.009 2 notation 05-9 from Table 5
Marathas (Table 5)	-948
	=920.009 2+948
Class No.	920.009 294 8

Migration of Panjabis	**304.800 899 142**
Base number	304.8

Standard subdivision	-089
Instruction	Add to base number -089 notation 05-9 from Table 5
Panjabis (Table 5)	-914 2
	=304.8+0089+914 2
Class No.	304.800 899 142

Elementary education of Pakistanis	**372.089 914 122**
Base number	372
Standard subdivision	-089
Instruction	Add to base number -089 notation 05-9 from Table 5
Pakistanis (Table 5)	-914 122
	=372+089+914 122
Class No.	372.089 914 122

Husband-wife relationship of Todas	**306.872 089 948 1**
Base number	306.872
Standard subdivision	-089
Instruction	Add to base number -089 notation 05-9 from Table 5
Todas (Table 5)	-948 1
	=306.872+089+948 1
Class No.	306.872 089 948 1

Higher education of Nepalis in India	**378.008 991 495 054**
Base number	378
Standard subdivision	-089

Instruction	Add to base number -089 notation 05-9 from Table 5
Nepalis (Table 5)	-914 95
Connecting digit	0
India (Table 2)	-54
	=378+008 9+914 95+0+54
Class No.	378.008 991 495 054

Journal of Ethno psychology of Italians in Japan **155.845 105 205**

Base number	155.84
Instruction	Add to base number 155.84 notation 05-9 from Table 5
Italians (Table 5)	-51
Connecting digit	0
Japan (Table 2)	-52
Journal (Table 1)	-05
	=155.84+51+0+52+05
Class No.	155.845 105 205

Encyclopaedia of Ethnic cookery of Paharis **641.592 914 960 03**

Base number	641.592
Instruction	Add to base number 641.592 notation 05-9 from Table 5
Paharis (Table 5)	-914 96
Encyclopaedia (Table 1)	-03
	=641.592+914 96+003
Class No.	641.592 914 960 03

Use of Table 5

(Note: Because after the notation from Table 5 there is no zero and notation from Table 2, hence double zeros are used for standard subdivisions)

Journal on Elementary education of Sri Lankans **372.089 914 13**

Base number 372

Standard subdivision -089

Instruction Add to base number -089 notation 05-9 from Table 5

Sri Lankans (Table 5) -914 13

=372+089+914 13

Class No. 372.089 914 13

(Note: As notation from Table 5 has been added through interposition of -089 from Table 1, hence standard subdivision is not added.)

Civil rights of Panjabi Indians **323.119 142**

Base number 323.11

Instruction Add to base number 323.11 notation 1-9 from Table 5

Panjabi (Table 5) -914 2

=323.11+914 2

Class No. 323.119 142

(Note: Preference is given to ethnic group.)

Civil rights of Pakistanis who become Indian citizen **323.119 141 22**

Base number 323.11

Instruction Add to base number 323.11 notation 1-9 from Table 5

Pakistanis (Table 5) -914 122

=323.11+914 122

Class No. 323.119 141 22

(Note: Preference is given to ancestral group.)

9

USE OF TABLE 6: LANGUAGES

Table 6 in DDC consists of notations for languages. Like other tables in DDC this table is also never used alone, but may be used with those numbers from the schedules and other tables to which the classifier is instructed to add notation from Table 6. Hence notation from Table 6 cannot be added without an instruction. The instructions regarding use of Table 6 are of two types viz. 1. Instructions in the schedule. 2. Instructions in the other tables. You have already used Table 6 while using Table 4. Let us try some more examples.

Libraries in the Tamil speaking regions	**027.017 594 811**
Base number	027.0
Instruction (at .01-.09)	Add to base number 027.0 notation 1-9 from Table 2
Regions where specific (Table 2) languages predominate	-175
Instruction	Add to base number -175 notation 1-9 from Table 6
Tamil language (Table 6)	948 11
	=027.0+175+948 11
Class No.	027.017 594 811

Journalism and newspapers in Kannada speaking regions	**079.175 948 14**

Base number	079
Instruction	Add to base number 079 notation 1-9 from Table 2
Regions where specific (Table 2) languages predominate	-175
Instruction	Add to base number -175 notation 1-9 from Table 6
Kannada language (Table 6)	948 14
	=079+175+948 14
Class No.	079.175 948 14

Economic history of Turkish speaking regions **330.917 594 35**

Base number	330.91
Instruction	Add to base number 330.91 the numbers following -1 in notation -11-19 from Table 2
Regions where specific (Table 2) languages predominate	-175
Instruction	Add to base number -175 notation 1-9 from Table 6
Turkish language (Table 6)	943 5
	=330.91+75+943 5
Class No.	330.917 594 35

Structural approach to expression of Russian for Malayalam speaking people **491.782 494 812**

Base number	491.7
Structural approach to expression for (Table 4)	-824
Persons whose native language is different	

Instruction	Add to -824 notation 2-9 from Table 6
Malayalam language (Table 6)	-948 12
	=491.7+824+948 12
Class No.	491.782 494 812

Audio-lingual approach to expression of Hindi for French speaking people **491.438 344 1**

Base number	491.43
Audio-lingual approach to expression for (Table 4)	-834
Persons whose native language is different	
Instruction	Add to -834 notation 2-9 from Table 6
French language (Table 6)	-41
	=491.43+834+41
Class No.	491.438 344 1

Kannada-language primer for peoples whose native language is Italian **494.814 864 51**

Base number	494.814
Readers for specific native (Table 4) language speakers	-864
Instruction	Add to -864 notation 2-9 from Table 6
Italian language (Table 6)	-51
	=494.814+864+51
Class No.	494.814 864 51

Swedish-Danish Dictionary **439.813 397**

Base number	439.81
Dictionary (Table 4)	-3
Instruction	Add to -3 notation 2-9 from Table 6
Swedish Language (Table 6)	-397
	=439.81+3+397
Class No.	439.813 397

Grahshobha: A Hindi monthly **059.914 31**

Base number	059
Instruction	Add to base number 059 notation 7-9 from Table 6
Hindi Language (Table 6)	-914 31
	=059+914 31
Class No.	059.914 31

General encyclopaedia in Sanskrit language **039.912**

Base number	039
Instruction	Add to base number 039 notation 7-9 from Table 6
Sanskrit Language (Table 6)	-912
	=039+912
Class No.	039.912

Translation of Bible in Telugu **220.594 827**

Base number	220.5
Instruction (at .53-59)	Add to base number 220.5 notation 3-9 from Table 6
Telugu Language (Table 6)	-948 27
	=220.5+948 27

Class No.	220.594 827

Translation of Bhagavad Gita in English	**294.592 404 521**
Base number	294.592 4
Translations	045
Instruction	Add to base number 045 notation 1-9 from Table 6
English Language (Table 6)	-21
	=294.592 4+045+21
Class No.	294.592 404 521

(Note: The instructions for classifying translations is provided with the help of * and footnote.)

General bibliographies of Gujarati language works	**011.291 47**
Base number	011.2
Instruction	Add to base number 011.2 notation 2-9 from Table 6
Gujarati Language (Table 6)	-914 7
	=011.2+914 7
Class No.	011.291 47

Teaching of French in Elementary schools	**372.654 1**
Base number	372.65
Instruction (at .552-.659)	Add to base number 372.65 notation 1-9 from Table 6
French Language (Table 6)	-41
	=372.65+41
Class No.	372.654 1

Folk literature in Oriya language	**398.204 914 56**
Base number	398.204
Instruction	Add to base number 398.204 notation 1-9 from Table 6
Oriya Language (Table 6)	-914 56
	=398.204+914 56
Class No.	398.204 914 56

Tamil Proverbs	**398.994 811**
Base number	398.9
Instruction	Add to base number 398.9 notation 1-9 from Table 6
Oriya Language (Table 6)	-948 11
	=398.9+948 11
Class No.	398.994 811

10

TREATMENT OF GROUPS OF PERSONS

Table 7 has been deleted from DDC 22. How the numbers, which were previously made by using Table 7 with the help of add instructions, are to be made is dealt in this chapter. The use of Table 7 is replaced by direct use of notation already available in the schedules and in notation 08 from Table 1. The following examples can make it easy to understand how these numbers are to be built?

Psychology for Surgeons	**150.246 17**
Base number	150
Instruction	150.1-.9 Standard subdivisions
The subject for persons in specific (Table 1) occupations	-024
Instruction	Add to base number -024 notation 001-999
Surgery	617
	=150+24+617
Class No.	150.24617

Digital Photography among Library classificationists	**775.088 025 42**
Base number	775
Standard subdivision	-088
Instruction	Add to base number -088

	notation 001-999
Library Classification	025.42
	= 775+088+025.42
Class No.	775.088 025 42

Proprietary libraries in Muslim countries	**027.217 67**
Base number	027.2
Instruction	Add to base number 027.2 notation 1-9 from Table 2
Regions where specific (Table 2) religions predominate	-176
Instruction	Add to base number -176 the numbers following 29 in 292-299
Islam	297
	=027.2+176+7
Class No.	027.217 67

Ethics of financial economists	**174.933 2**
Base number	174.9
Instruction	Add to base number 174.9 notation 001-999
Financial economics	332
	=174.9+332
Class No.	174.933 2

Opinions of electronics engineering	**303.388 021 381**
Base number	303.388

Instruction	Add to base number 303.388 notation 001-999
Electronics engineering	621.381
	=303.388+621.381
Class No.	303.388 621 381

Women pilots	**305.436 291 309 2**
Base number	305.43
Instruction	Add to base number 305.43 notation 001-999
Pilots	629.130 92
	=305.43+629.130 92
Class No.	305.436 291 309 2

Christian scientists in Canada	**305.689 571**
Base number	305.6
Instruction	Add to base number 305.6 the numbers following 2 in 230-299
Christian scientist	289.5
Instruction	Add to base number 289.5 notation 4-9 from Table 2
Canada (Table 2)	-71
	=305.6+895+71
Class No.	305.689 571

Air mail workers	**305.938 314 4**
Base number	305.9
Instruction	Add to base number 305.9 notation 100-999

Airmail	383.144
	=305.9+383.144
Class No.	305.938 314 4
Customs of surgeons	**390.461 7**
Base number	390.4
Instruction	Add to base number 390.4 notation 001-999
Surgeons (Surgery)	617
	=390.4+617
Class No.	390.461 7
Muslim sacred music	**781.77**
Base number	781.7
Instruction	Add to base number 781.7 the numbers following 29 in 294-299
Islam	~~29~~7
	=781.7+7
Class No.	781.77
Composition of preludes for Buddhist services	**782.343 089 281 3**
Base number	782.3
Instruction	Add to base number 782.3 the numbers following 29 in 294-299; then add further as follows
Buddhism	~~29~~4.3
Musical form	08
Instruction	Add to 08 the numbers

	following 784.18 in 784.182-784.189
Preludes	~~781.18~~9 28
Instruction	Add as instructed under 781.2-781.8
General principles	Add to 1 numbers following 781 in 781.1-781.7
Composition	~~781~~.3
	=782.3+43+08+929+1+3
Class No.	782.343 089 291 3
Collections of letters on lawyers	**808.869 352 834**
Base number	808.869
Instruction	Add to base number 808.869 notation 1-3 from Table 3C
Kinds of persons (Table 3C)	-352
Instruction	Add to -352 the numbers following-08 in 081-089 from Table 1
Specific occupational groups (Table 1)	~~-08~~8
Instruction	Add to base number -088 notation 001-999
Law (Schedule)	340
	=808.869+352+8+34
Class No.	808.869 352 834
Collections of Slavic novels by Cricketers	**891.830 080 921 796 358**
Base number	891.8

Novels (Table 3B)	-3
Instruction	Add to -300 as instructed under-1-8.
Coll.ctions displaying specific features	801-809
Instruction	Add to 80 notation 1-9 from Table 3C
Literature for and by persons of specific (Table 3C) occupations	- 921
Instruction	Add to-921 notation 001-999
Cricket (Schedule)	796.358
	=891.8+300+80+921+796.358
Class No.	891.830 080 921 796 358